BIG
&
BEAUTIFUL

BIG
&
BEAUTIFUL

CHALLENGING THE MYTHS AND CELEBRATING OUR SIZE

Margaret Greaves

GRAFTON BOOKS
A Division of the Collins Publishing Group

LONDON GLASGOW
TORONTO SYDNEY AUCKLAND

Grafton Books
A Division of the Collins Publishing Group
8 Grafton Street, London W1X 3LA

Published by Grafton Books 1990

Copyright © Margaret Greaves 1990

British Library Cataloguing in Publication Data
Greaves, Margaret
Big and beautiful: challenging the myths and
celebrating our size.
1. Women. Body. Psychosocial aspects
I. Title
305.4

ISBN 0–246–13384–8
ISBN 0–246–13385–6 (Pbk)

Photoset in Palatino by Deltatype, Ellesmere Port
Printed in Great Britain by
Hartnolls Ltd, Bodmin, Cornwall.

All rights reserved. No part of this publication may be reproduced, stored in a retrieval system, or transmitted, in any form or by any means, electronic, mechanical, photocopying, recording or otherwise, without the prior permission of the publisher.

CONTENTS

	Acknowledgements	6
	Introduction	7
1	Attitudes and Prejudices	13
2	The Perpetrators	23
3	Images in Perspective	48
4	The Myths Exposed	69
5	Good Inside	90
6	Feeling Fit	115
7	In Your Own Fashion	136
8	Fighting Back	148
	APPENDICES	
I	Nutrition	157
II	Useful addresses	163
III	Bibliography	167
	Index	171

ACKNOWLEDGEMENTS

With special thanks to all my friends at Spectrum for their love and encouragement, but especially to Rex Bradley, Terry Cooper and Jenner Roth, without whose consistent, caring confrontation and enthusiastic support over the years it would have been impossible for me to write this book anyway!

And lastly to my darling husband Brian for his constant love and practical support throughout the writing process.

INTRODUCTION

For as long as I can remember, I have struggled with my body. Even as a child, I felt overweight, yet looking back at childhood photographs I was not at all fat. I was large – five foot nine by the time I was thirteen, with big bones, a large frame, always long-limbed and always the tallest in the class – but I was certainly not fat. To fit in with the ideal image of the time, however, I wanted my body to be tiny. I felt as if I was taking up too much space in the world and I wanted to shrink.

My body has always exceeded the accepted height/weight ratios, even when I was at my thinnest and not carrying an ounce of excess fat. Nor has it ever been easy for me to dress in ready-to-wear clothes, because of my large frame and my height. Mine is the kind of body which gains weight easily and it would put up a tremendous battle whenever I forced it to suffer hardship and deprivation in a vain attempt to lose a few pounds

At the age of seventeen I climbed on to the dieting carousel, worried that I was heavy and big in the hip, and I managed to bring my weight down to ten stone six. I was still only eleven stone two when I married at the age of twenty, with a 36/24/38 figure, but for a long time I continued to feel fat and unattractive, and therefore continued to diet.

A few years ago I gave up that struggle and, after a lot of hard work, therapy and personal change, I learned to listen to my body and to feel comfortable within it, eating nutritiously rather than starving myself on punitive diets. I felt good about myself. Then I looked around and realized that the rest of the world still thought there was something wrong with me because of my size. I began to challenge that view and met considerable hostility. This came not only from thin people; large women also were distrustful because I was not talking like a victim, saying that it was my fault I did not fit the conventional ideal image. On the contrary, I was saying that I did not see why there should be an ideal image at all, that I thought it was ridiculous, that the person inside the body was far more important than the body itself anyway, and that there was no reason on earth why I should conform to society's ideal image when I knew that I was fine as *me*.

In the course of my work as a psychotherapist I started talking to other large women who were judging themselves severely for being the size they were and who accepted society's attitudes to largeness. I began to run groups for them; I set up workshops designed to help them accept their size and channel their energies into more important matters than dieting, by encouraging them to recognize and develop their assets and talents rather than fret about food.

I soon learned that my story was shared by them all:

there were those who had trodden the same path; they had looked at themselves and, like me, had struggled against being affected by what people told them. They had fought to ignore subconscious negative feelings about their large bodies; they had eventually won their internal battles and emerged at the fragile stage of feeling comfortable within their own skins, only to be faced with prejudices which claimed that if they really had sorted themselves out they would be thin, and assumed that because they remained large they still had problems.

That attitude is an insult to large women. Nobody automatically has personal problems because, for instance, they are black or white, or middle class or working class, or male or female – or large or thin. Some people in all these sections of society undoubtedly do have problems but it is not a prerequisite of any of them. People would be outraged if it was suggested that all women had problems, or all black people had problems, and certainly sexism and racism are being widely challenged now. It is equally unjust to label large women as having problems simply because they are large.

Some valiant work was done in the late 1970s and early 1980s by writers such as Susie Orbach, author of *Fat is a Feminist Issue*, who encouraged a better understanding of eating disorders, yet the book still carries the implication that if you are large you have a problem. Orbach suggests that when a woman has solved her eating disorders, then she will feel comfortable with her own body and arrive at a 'normal' weight.

It is totally wrong that this expectation should be laid on us. All the women I have met who are large and who have experienced a lifetime of punitive dieting have found that not only did the weight return once they relaxed the regime but also that their bodies settled at higher weights than before, so that they needed to diet again in order to return to a pre-diet weight. Every woman who diets regularly recognizes the plateau, the point at which the body really puts up a fight against the abuse of dieting. Dieting in the way that I did, and many other large women do, is to go into battle with your own body. I believe (and research is beginning to support this belief) that the body protects itself in this battle by increasing its normal weight each time, almost as an insurance against future threats to its well-being.

One of the main aims of this book is to help large women who have been engaged in this struggle to stop fighting. It will encourage you to nurture and love your body rather than do battle with it. Any movement towards change needs to be done with self-respect and care, not with disgust and self-rejection. Doing battle with your body is not the answer and I would like to think that young women who may be about to start fighting will read this book and recognize that dieting and punitive measures are self-defeating.

Through this book I hope to highlight the prejudiced attitudes towards large women – and I concentrate on women because their problems are more complex than those of large men. I shall examine why those attitudes persist and in what ways they are perpetuated. I shall look at the historical perspective: how the ideal images of women's bodies have changed through the ages and the extent to which women have contorted themselves to conform to the current model. At first glance these fashions for ideal shapes seem to change almost on a whim but I shall describe how factors like national prosperity play an important role.

Whatever the shape fashion decrees, a lot of money is invested in persuading women to abuse their bodies in order to conform with the contemporary ideal. There is a huge industry encouraging us to become thinner with pills and potions, dietary aids, surgery, slimming clubs, 'fitness' and 'health' organizations and so on, all making good profits out of women who are desperately unhappy with their bodies and who are trying to squeeze them into today's ideal mould.

The media support this industry. How often, for example, do you see a large woman in a serious role in plays and films? Indeed, wherever we look it is virtually impossible to see a positive role model for large women. Instead, they are seen as greedy, lazy, lacking in self-control, unhealthy, and as a problem in general.

That view *must* be challenged. This book is therefore addressed not only to large women but also to society as a whole, to people who make judgements and assumptions about size, who are influenced (just as much as large women are) by the prejudices and attitudes with which we are all bombarded. It is time that we all questioned the ways in which the media, the fashion industry and commercial concerns promote the ideal image in order to make financial gain. It is time we all became more aware of the prejudices against large women and examined our personal attitudes. I want to open people's eyes to their own prejudices, to inform and then to challenge them to change their false perceptions. Perhaps it will also help those large men who suffer from the thoughtlessness of others.

However, I am not putting forward a case for large women as victims, because those who blame others for their own situation render themselves incapable of doing much about it. The only realistic way to make changes, if that is what you want to do, is through self-love, self-nourishment and bringing together the body and the mind. When we love ourselves and our bodies, we are in a better position to make decisions about who we are and how we want to be in the world. I shall look at constructive ways in which women can change their own attitude towards themselves and then suggest positive ways of applying pressure to change other people's misconceptions as well. There are many practical difficulties for a large person in a society which does not cater for size but we can apply pressure for change in the world around us and take steps to counteract the problems faced by large women every day.

1

ATTITUDES AND PREJUDICES

In February 1988, an article by Neville Hodgkinson in the *Sunday Times* reported on a study carried out by Medical Research Council doctors at the Dunn Nutrition Unit in Cambridge. Their research showed quite clearly that body size is connected with personal metabolism. At its simplest, some people are easygoing and will be large, while others will remain thin however much they eat. Babies destined to grow into large people eat at more or less the same rate as other babies, but they are more placid and expend less energy while awake, and therefore they burn off fewer calories. American researchers have independently reached the same conclusion: those who are fat do not necessarily eat more than other people; they often burn fewer calories, not because they are lazy but because they are either genetically or habitually tuned to a lower metabolic rate.

The article was specific about the metabolic link, but the newspaper's readers were sceptical and their letters in the following week's issue revealed their prejudices. One woman described how she had queued up at a supermarket check-out behind overweight customers with overweight offspring trundling tell-tale trolleys laden with unsuitable food. Another woman said that, despite the research, she still firmly believed that over-eating was the cause of obesity and she cited her 'grossly overweight' husband as an example, saying that he never ate one biscuit at a time but a quarter of the packet, never one piece of chocolate but the whole bar, and that he had cheerfully eaten second helpings of both courses of his Sunday lunch while he gloated over the paper's article. She demanded that the scientists should think again because, she said, 'This research does nothing to help us control our fatties.'

What right has she to 'control fatties', or anyone else? Her attitude is all too common. It seems that it is acceptable for the world and his wife to tell large people how much food they should eat, how much they should weigh and what they should do with their lives – a situation which the 'average' person would neither expect nor tolerate. When you are large, however, you begin to expect such criticism and interference.

Nor does it come only from members of the family. A woman who attended one of my workshops was approached at work by a superior who indicated that she should lose weight; she was led to believe that, unless she did so, her chances of promotion would be jeopardized or that she might lose her job altogether. When she pursued the matter, she was told that her weight was greater than that found acceptable for her height according to the standard actuarial charts used by the insurance industry, that she was thus considered an insurance risk (it was claimed that her size increased her chances of an early death) and that therefore her employer would be required to pay a higher premium on her behalf. When I last heard from her, she was fighting the situation by contacting her union and solicitor, but this reaction immediately placed her in the category of a 'difficult' employee. It may be that this will create such an awkward atmosphere at work that she will want to leave the job anyway.

Incidentally, the 'scientific' basis of those standard insurance charts (which were originally drawn up by the Metropolitan Life Insurance Company in the United States) is now being questioned and revised. Their misleading criteria are looked at in more detail in Chapter 4.

There are other problems in the workplace. There is the notion that large people take more time off work for health reasons, but there is no supporting evidence for this belief. Then there is the assumption that a large woman cannot look smart enough for a front-office job, or cannot be glamorous enough to work, say, as an air hostess. A particularly insidious form of discrimination is practised by large companies who provide uniforms up to size 14 or 16 and then claim that it is not possible to employ larger people because the uniforms would not fit them. Then there is the chocolate factory which will employ large women on the factory floor, but not in the front offices or reception areas in case the public makes a damaging association between the product and the women's size.

The assumption which links food consumption with body size is widespread, and fatness is often defined as the sign of an eating disorder. Large people are generally stereotyped as being greedy, but while some of them do indeed eat compulsively, or inappropriately, that does not mean to say that all large people do so, any more than it would be true to say that all thin people are suffering from anorexia nervosa. In reality many eat no more (and often less) than anyone else. Yet the fact remains that large people are usually seen as having no control over their eating habits. It is assumed that they will want big helpings, for example, or will overindulge in unsuitable snacks. This encourages large people to be furtive about eating. Many large women hesitate to eat in public; many of them feel so insecure because of the ridicule their size attracts that they go out of their way to prove they are *not* greedy and automatically alter their behaviour to suit different situations.

Because large people are thought to be greedy, this lack of control is assumed to extend to the rest of their lives. They are often seen as lazy, self-indulgent, lacking in fitness and incapable of looking good or of achieving success personally, in a career, or even in family life.

The subject of dieting, and the failure of various diets, is a common topic of conversation among women, especially over a meal-table, yet if a woman actually shows signs of losing weight, whether by dieting or by other means, then her friends will not on the whole give her their support. An element of competition arises between women, though they might not be prepared to admit it, and the woman who has lost some of her weight can be seen as a sexual threat to friends who no longer trust her in the company of their husbands. (Personally, I would not want as a friend a woman who assumed I was no such threat because of my size!) Subconsciously, people seem to believe that she is no longer the same woman and that, by losing size, she has not only become more attractive to men but has also somehow changed as a person and perhaps become something of a stranger with whom her friends no longer feel at ease. That reaction is, of course, as ridiculous as believing that a personality is altered when a person's reflection is seen in a distorting mirror at the funfair.

The common public misconception that a large woman is 'out of control' is reflected in the media where those with a good image are rarely large. Large people are bad, comical or to be ridiculed. It is hard to find any positive characters among large women on television or in the cinema who do not wish to reduce their weight; usually they are classified as odd, asexual, sexually unattractive or sexually voracious. I explore this in more detail in Chapter 2.

It was not always thus. Historically, large women have been fêted as attractive, sexual and much sought-after; but society is quick to judge, criticize and oppress people who do not fit into the currently acceptable norm, and such norms can change. Today the acceptable image is thin – sometimes unhealthily thin – and many women seem to be almost frightened of fat. In the UK and in the USA, studies consistently show that the physical factors which carry the greatest stigma are skin colour and excess body fat. (Relevant studies by S. J. Chetwynd, *et al.*, and by Susan and Orland Wooley are listed in the Bibliography.) But racism and sizeism (or 'fat-o-phobia') differ in that people cannot do much about the colour of the skin they are born with, whereas it is assumed that weight can and should be under voluntary control and that there is some choice in the matter.

Kim Chernin, in her book *Woman Size: The Tyranny of Slenderness*, quotes a startling article from a 1981 issue of the *San Francisco Chronicle*: 'In this era when inflation has assumed alarming proportions and the threat of nuclear war has become a serious danger, when violent crime is on the increase and unemployment a persistent social fact, 500 people were asked by pollsters what they fear most in the world. 190 of them answered that their greatest fear is "getting fat".' How on earth have our priorities become so distorted?

This obsession against fat reflects the way in which women have been valued and rewarded for their appearance rather than for their true worth, and the discrimination against fat women should serve as a reminder to all of us that we need to change the criteria against which society assesses its appreciation of women.

While thinness is judged to be acceptable, it is easy to see how the stigma of excess weight limits a woman's social and economic opportunities. Unfortunately, instead of viewing sizeism as *society's* problem, many women internalize the fear and intolerance of fat as their personal problem. Instead of trying to change society, they try to change themselves, punishing and hating their bodies, and spending money on various diets and health programmes.

Thin women, as well as fat, can be obsessed in this way, but there is a crucial difference between a thin woman's dissatisfaction in not matching the impossibly thin ideal and the harassment and discrimination experienced by large women. The crux of the difference is that a thinner woman will be acceptable to society even though she herself is unhappy with her size. Unlike men, who see themselves as a whole (mind and body), women tend to identify themselves very clearly with their bodies and are therefore very critical of their appearance. Society is taught that women and their bodies are one and the same thing. Almost every woman dislikes some part of her body and would like to change or hide that part, but a thin woman, however imperfect she finds her body, is socially acceptable. Should she talk about her dissatisfaction, the social response is usually something like: 'Oh, but you are fine, my dear – I can't understand why you feel like that.' A large woman is unlikely to talk about her body at all, because she has probably learned to anticipate comments which inevitably indicate how unacceptable her size is. Well-meaning people will harass her with advice on diets and self-control.

Thus the difference between the large woman and the thinner woman is that the latter's dissatisfaction with her body is not upheld by society – quite the opposite – and if she talks about it she is likely to be reassured. In the unlikely event of a large woman talking about her dissatisfaction, then she will be given affirmation that her dissatisfaction is justified – which is no boost at all to her self-esteem.

Surely people have a right to be the size they are and to choose how they behave? The general fear and hatred of fat should not lead to discrimination against large people merely because they do not fit contemporary ideals. Society, however, persists in its strong prejudices based on outward appearances – race, colour, age, sex, height, clothing or hairstyle and, of course, size – and with size the discrimination begins at a very early age. Large children are ridiculed in the playground and in the changing-room, and teachers assume they will not want to be involved in games. One woman in my workshop was asked by her daughter not to collect her from school any more because her friends were teasing her about her fat mother.

Oppression, discrimination and thoughtlessness are evident in many areas of a large person's life. Public places, for instance, are not designed to make things easier for those who are larger than the norm. Seats in planes and cinemas are crowded together without a thought for the larger frame; in restaurants it is increasingly the practice to anchor the seats to the floor so that there is only a restricted space between chair and table; and in pubs, too, space is often limited. I have known women refuse to go into certain places for fear of the embarrassment of not being able to sit down at the table. On buses and trains, the last empty seat to be taken will be the one next to a large person because people do not want to feel crowded. In hospitals there is the embarrassment of your naked body being partially exposed in public because the edges of the gown will not meet, and this can make an ordeal out of a simple visit for an X-ray.

One of the problems is that large people are seen as taking up too much space, especially if they are women. A man 'is'; a woman has to pay a price in order to gain the right to exist. She is often very apologetic about being on this planet at all. Her body must be acceptable before she herself can be accepted. She is not supposed to take up space in the world and it appears that people feel a need to ridicule her in order to put her down or reduce her to an appropriate size so that she is less of a physical threat. Maybe this is one reason why so many large women dread the summertime, when their bodies will be more than usually exposed to the harsh public gaze and there is nowhere to hide.

There can be problems for large women in general exercise classes where some of the exercises are physically awkward because of the woman's shape (rather than because of her size) or because her personal level of progress, with certain types of aerobic exercise in particular, does not correlate with the general ability level required. Whatever the reason, she is not suited to the exercise and her anticipation of ridicule in such a class tends to deter her from joining in or continuing with a series of sessions. On the other hand, if large women are segregated into special classes because of their size, their feelings of oppression increase, though it is different if they have chosen to organize such a class themselves.

The problem is exacerbated by the widespread assumption that large people, especially large women, are not interested in activities like dancing and do not want to be involved in any kind of exercise or sport anyway; it is certainly assumed that they will not want to wear clothes suitable for active pursuits. Sports clothes in general are rarely available in larger sizes; when they are, the choice is depressingly restricted, or else the clothes are very expensive indeed. This situation is slowly improving, but there is a very long way to go and in the meantime a large woman who is already self-conscious about her ability to perform an exercise adequately is further demoralized by her inability to find appropriate clothes.

Nor is it only sports clothes. Personal appearance is important to the self-confidence of most women, whatever their size, but there is still a supposition that large women cannot look good and therefore need not be taken into account by the fashion industry. It is rare to find a fashion feature which automatically includes clothes for large women and when it does the focus is on clothes which will 'improve' the look, i.e. make a woman look thinner.

Who is to say that large women *want* to look thinner, or that they should look thinner? We are back to the central theme of society deciding what is acceptable, criticizing people who do not conform, and setting out to control them.

2

THE PERPETRATORS

How is it that these attitudes and prejudices are perpetrated? Among those who keep the myths alive are, ironically, women who have themselves faced prejudice because of their size and who fear that their daughters will inherit similar problems.

Mothers of large babies are often subjected to unkind and hurtful criticism: assumptions are made that the child is being overfed, or fed inappropriately, although very often this is not the case. When she hears remarks like, 'Oh, what a large baby – isn't she chubby!', a young mother may interpret them as implying that the child is fat and oversize. Yet it would be very strange if a baby who weighed perhaps nine pounds at birth was not a large child at six months old.

In our efforts to help and protect our children against the knocks of the world, it is all too easy to initiate rather than allay the problem. Families often sow the seeds of self-doubt in children, and the doubt can grow into lack of self-esteem, a low evaluation of oneself, and a fear of being generally unacceptable. In trying to protect a large child from prejudice, some mothers actually create feelings of inadequacy by behaving as if size or weight *is* a problem, when it need not be. Children pick up how we feel about the way they behave, think and look – whether at a subconscious level or from straightforward messages consciously given. If a parent is unhappy about having a large child, however well-intentioned that concern might be, then the child will absorb the parental doubt and begin to feel unhappy about itself. If a girl senses that her mother cannot accept her as she is, then she feels there must be something wrong with her – something much more fundamental than her size.

Very often this realization is heightened by the mother's expressions of anxiety, for example by her suggestion that the child should not have second helpings because she knows that other people will make jokes or comments about it. The mother's concern is also betrayed in the way she dresses the child to make her look smaller or thinner – dark colours, loose clothing, all-in-one swimsuits to hide the body, dresses which hang straight from a yoke rather than being nipped in at the waist. To disguise her size, a daughter is dressed differently from other children: she is put into vertical stripes or an enveloping smock instead of that pretty pink frilly dress she longs for, and she immediately feels set apart from other girls.

Many of the women I have spoken to share my own sense that, as children, we had to wear something different because our bodies needed to be hidden. This was all done from love but it immediately set us apart from other children. Looking back, this is often recognized as the time when a woman first realizes that she is not acceptable, and the mother who sought to protect and help her has in fact increased the difficulties which so often have to be faced. Large children will anyway come under stress among their contemporaries: their size sets them apart just as the very small child, or anyone else who does not conform to the average, is seen as 'different'.

But let us focus on those large children. They are likely to be teased about their size; they are likely to be called names like 'Fatty'; if they are seen to eat a single chocolate bar or a cream cake, it will be assumed that they always eat that sort of food. They are identified with characters like Billy Bunter and treated as the odd one out in any group, expected to be lazy, unfit and out of breath, although large children are not necessarily any of those things.

It is of course natural for mothers to want their children to be acceptable and many believe that acceptance demands conformity, including conformity to the 'ideal' size. The implication to the child is that if her size is 'normal', then everything else about her will be acceptable too. Some parents deliberately buy clothes a size too small for a teenager as an incentive for her to lose weight, and as an adult she will buy small for the same reason.

Sometimes young people spend years trying to attain an acceptable size and in the process they wait to live, not taking part in sport, not buying the clothes they want, not doing what they want to do because they might be laughed at, or they think they are not worth it, until they are an 'acceptable' size. Sometimes mothers put young people on stringent diets, and take them on an endless round of child psychologists, dieticians and doctors, and in the process the children become increasingly less sure of themselves and more and more convinced that they are abnormal.

Many mothers still believe that a daughter's happiness lies in getting married, settling down, having children and a good sex life, and that therefore she must be sexually acceptable in order to attract a husband. Conversely, being large can also be used as a test of love: if a large woman is loved in spite of her size, in some way that proves to her that she is loved for herself, not merely for sexual beauty.

According to Freudian concepts, women suffer from weak psychological boundaries: they have trouble knowing where they begin and where they end, or how much 'psychological space' they take up in the world. Being large seems to help some women to define their space. We all need a private, personal retreat for nourishment and recovery, a place of our own, and fat can become an indirect way of creating this personal space. It can also act as a buffer against the demands of others: it can be a shield behind which a woman can conceal herself, as women have always tried to defend themselves in what seems so often to be a hostile world. Some women hide behind cosmetics, others may take up body-building and others take comfort in their bulk. All these strategies are a form of disguise and protection.

Susie Orbach, in *Fat is a Feminist Issue*, agrees that some women subconsciously gain weight as layers of protection: they *want* to be undesirable and nonsexual, and their weight is a cocoon which shields them from men's sexual advances and saves them from having to handle their own sexuality. When thinness is equated with beauty and therefore sexual desirability, being large can be used to create a barrier between the sexual and non-sexual self; once a woman has opted out of the beauty stakes by being large, she can trade in part of the power of beauty for power of a different kind. She is more likely to be dealt with directly as a person: men will consider her actions and what she is saying rather than be distracted by their enjoyment of looking at her and anticipating sexual favours. Very few large women are accused of sleeping their way to the top. As Rita Friedman says in her book *Beauty Bound*: 'Like the eunuch who roams freely through the harem without threatening the sheikh's property, an overweight "asexual" woman can sometimes enjoy opportunities not available to her thinner sisters.'

In a more negative manner, Wendy Chapkis (*Beauty Secrets: Women and the Politics of Appearance*) quotes a woman as saying that, when fat, 'I don't want to have sex and I expect my fat to say it for me', while another woman claimed that she made herself fat and ugly 'because I couldn't stand the way men were treating women who were pretty'.

There is some truth in this and I have certainly met women whose size varies according to how good they feel about themselves – not just sexually but generally. Quite often (though not necessarily) a woman finds that, once she accepts herself and feels comfortable with herself, her size becomes stable or may even reduce to some extent, sometimes to a level that society would consider 'normal'. But one must beware of assuming that all women are large because they have psychological and sexual problems, or that all large women feel bad about themselves. Most women have difficulties in coping with other people's attitudes to them, and they may react with anger or frustration, or succumb to despair, but it is clearly misleading to suggest that being large is always a protection and that when a woman no longer feels vulnerable her protective layers will just melt away.

Incidentally, although it is claimed that 'fat is a feminist issue' and that 'fat is a metaphor for feeling powerless', it is a sad fact that many large women who believed that they would find acceptance within the feminist movement have in practice found much the same attitudes there as everywhere else. They are still not accepted for themselves, and many have been hurt and disillusioned by that. In the book *Shadow on a Tightrope*, Laurie Lepoff wrote a piece on 'Fat Politics' in which she tried to explain how pained she was by attitudes to her size among those who had supported her as a lesbian. Women in the lesbian community usually give each other enormous support against the discrimination that they inevitably meet because of their sexuality; they give each other a sense of strength, power, beauty and, vitally, anger. Lepoff, uplifted by that support, was particularly distressed to find that her friends' attitudes to her size were as prejudiced, discriminatory and oppressive as those of the rest of society. Lesbian women seemed to look for slim partners and they perpetuated the misconception that size was a matter of choice and that a large woman should be able to control her own weight. She said sadly that she felt more solidarity with a fat suburban housewife in this respect than with her slender lesbian sisters, although she added that she could expect as much support from that housewife as she could from a closet lesbian who believed herself to be sick and perverted. She would expect sizeism in society at large, although she could not condone it, but that it should also be rife in a community which had otherwise been so supportive and understanding was unexpected and particularly painful.

In any case, assumptions seem to be made about large women and sex, although there are of course all sorts of different sexual appetites which have nothing to do with a person's size. However, one common myth seems to be that all large women are non-sexual creatures who could not possibly be attractive to anyone, and men in relationships with large women often face an unspoken assumption (which may for all I know be a spoken one between men in the locker-room) that their sex life must be dull or non-existent. The alternative myth is the Earth Mother image: a large woman with big breasts is assumed to be very sexual, or so desperate for sex that she will accept anybody, and thus large women become the butt of innuendo and harassment.

The Earth Mother quality seems to be permissible in someone who cares. In my own work as a therapist, I find that some people are attracted by my size because they think I will mother them; others are surprised that anybody in my position (as a successful, dynamic, self-employed career woman with a happy family life) could be my size because they assume that large women cannot feel happy about themselves. Then there are women who have spent a lifetime despairing of themselves and who come to Big and Beautiful workshops and say, 'Oh, how I'd like to be like you!' I tell them they can be, and they begin to see me as a positive role model because, 'If Margaret can do it, then so can I.' On the other hand, I sometimes find in my work for various organizations that people with whom I have previously had telephone conversations will visibly falter when they first meet me face to face: they are obviously surprised at my size because it does not fit the image they have of me and I do not fit the stereotype. The unspoken feeling seems to be that if I am a professional businesswoman, successful in my work, I should be slim and neat. But someone like Claire Rayner, who is certainly large, is respected and welcomed on the television screen for her knowledge and for her skills in helping people: she is seen as the ultimate caring Earth Mother. Erin Pizzey is another example.

In general, however, there is a dearth of positive role models for large woman in the media. When did you last see a well-proportioned, shapely woman in an advertisement, for instance? Women considered desirable enough to sell a product are always thin, and the media in general reflect social prejudices by decreeing that 'fat is wrong'. Most women of my size in the world of entertainment are not considered desirable – unlike the view in the latter part of the 19th century and the early part of this century. Florrie Forde, a famous music-hall singer and a great pantomime artiste, was known for songs like 'Hold your hand out, naughty boy', 'Down at the Old Bull and Bush' and wartime favourites like 'It's a long way to Tipperary' and 'Pack up your troubles'. Busby's *British Music Hall: an illustrated who's who* says of Florrie Forde: 'She was the darling of the old school which considered that from bosom to thigh principal boys could not be too massive.' In those days, it would appear that size was a valuable attribute rather than a disadvantage.

Today, large women on stage are more likely to be comedians than 'darlings' and in general it seems that large women are easier to laugh at. Marjorie Rea, for example, is a semi-professional from Belfast who has been performing since she was a teenager, initially as a singer and increasingly as a stand-up comic. In *The Joke's On Us* by Morwena Banks and Amanda Swift, Marjorie Rea is described thus:

> She is gloriously portly and unselfconscious about it, cracking jokes about her weight and diet, as well as her husband, her driving and her Ulster accent. She looks as if she enjoys being on stage and intersperses her jokes with a magnificent wheezing cackle. Again, this is not avant-garde or high-tension stand-up; it works in a community with shared experiences among people who are relaxed and prepared to show their appreciation.

Unfortunately, I believe that while large women continue to behave in the way that Marjorie Rea does the stereotype of being large and jolly and making fun of yourself is perpetuated. This may be her way of portraying her humour, and she has a right to do so, but it does underpin the stereotype which causes many women who are large in a society where the ideal is thin to find themselves dealt with unfairly.

Norma J. Gravely, in her essay entitled 'Sexist humour as a form of social control – or – unfortunately – the joke is usually on us', says that humour is a social mechanism and one of the functions of joke-telling and appreciation is social control. She quotes La Fave: 'A joke is often humorous to the extent that it enhances an object of affection and/or disparages an object of repulsion, unhumorous to the extent that it does the opposite.' Typically, white heterosexual male comedians will tell a joke to prove the superiority of their own social group over a group considered inferior by reason of, say, sex, status or race. The 'superior' group's use of jokes to dominate the socially 'inferior' group often betrays an awareness that the feeling of superiority is unfounded and unjustifiable.

Looking more specifically at gender in this context, Gravely suggests: 'Men could perceive women or the autonomy of women as a threat to their basic security – their power, "rightness", importance and position. It could be quite threatening to those in power to foresee competition or possibly overthrow from a group – quite obviously equal in capability, intelligence, strength and energy – that had been maintained in subordination by methods of social control. The motivation would be strong enough to counteract any tendency towards assertiveness, independence and autonomy with even stronger controls.'

When women find themselves the butt of sexist jokes by men, they often land in a *Catch*-22 situation. If they stay in the assigned roles, they are devalued by the humour, and if they move outside those roles then they are put down with jokes. It is unusual for a woman to break out of this kind of social control by refusing to be the butt of the joke and instead making her own jokes directed at her own victims. Women who do successfully challenge the stereotypes today are women who, like Victoria Wood, write or control their own material in order to be humorous in their own way.

I don't see the answer as being for women comedians to retaliate with sexist humour of their own, and I certainly don't see it in their directing humour against themselves as large women in the style of Marjorie Rea. Although Gravely deals generally with the position of women in society, I believe that large women in society are placed in an even more 'inferior' social group than women in general and that it is dangerous for large female comedians to set them up as sitting targets for jokes, even if the motives are self-protective.

The authors of *The Joke's On Us* asked Victoria Wood: 'How do you feel about comedy as a woman?' Her reply was:

> I do find it an impossible question, 'how do you feel as a woman?', well, I've never been a man. And in terms of 'has it been harder?', well I've got no terms of comparison. I've never lived twice. Or lived once as a man and once as a woman. I truly believe that there is no sex discrimination in comedy because I don't believe the audience is interested. I don't believe there is any prejudice from the audience. I think that the prejudice is from the press. I know that there are fewer women in comedy, or in stand-up, say. But I don't believe any audience has ever gone, 'Oh God, she's a woman, I'm not going to laugh.' I don't think there's a problem because I think personality transcends gender in comedy.

In my opinion it is because of this belief, and because she writes or controls her own material, that Victoria Wood is nationally admired and respected as a comedian. She manages to use her personality rather than her gender or her size to fulfil the role that she wants to play in the world.

Working in radio eliminates the worries that many

larger female comedy performers have about their on-stage appearance. If their size is unknown to the audience, then the voice will portray whatever character is required and the audience can use their imaginations to fill in the appearance. Hattie Jacques, however, who was a large woman, was cast as the 'Fat Person' in *ITMA*. She is quoted in *The ITMA Years* by Ted Kavanagh as saying:

> It was planned that I should play a character 'Ella Phant'. Ted thought the laughs would come on the size gags but, being radio, and coupled with the fact that my voice didn't have the timbre of a 'heavy' person, that didn't really work out. It wasn't until one show when Tommy was supposed to be passing through a department store and knocked a speaking doll (me) that the audience reacted favourably. A large body with a very little voice seemed to hit the spot, so 'Sophie Tuckshop' was born – the terrible child who never stopped eating, with sickening results.

The radio audience in those days had no idea what Hattie Jacques looked like and were simply laughing because the jokes were about someone fat. This sort of characterization perpetuates the stereotyping of large women eating too much, therefore being greedy and also being figures of fun.

When Barbara Windsor was appearing in the TV series *The Rag Trade*, she felt that all she was asked to do was chew gum and say, 'Shh, here comes Mr Fenner.' She went to Dennis Main Wilson, the producer, to complain and he said, 'You're too attractive to be funny. In this country you have got to look like Hattie Jacques, Irene Handl or Thora Hird.'

Barbara Windsor did manage to be humorous in the *Carry On* films, by being 'flighty'. As Eleanor Bron said about situation comedy: 'Women are limited in their comedy: they have to be grotesque or flighty. Their parts are always directly to do with being a woman. In *Last of the Summer Wine* the men are characters but the women are either sex objects or harridans.'

The *Carry On* films made full use of these stereotypes, with frumpy women whom nobody fancied because they were big and fearsome (like Hattie Jacques) and the sexy, glamorous, 'flighty' parts played by Barbara Windsor. Joan Sims, incidentally, started off playing the flighty glamour parts and ended up playing the frumps. There were also charlady characters played by people like Irene Handl, or the angry wives and mothers-in-law played by Thora Hird and Dandy Nichols, all of whom would have been considered on the large side and who were caricatures and therefore seen as funny.

In *The Joke's On Us* Miriam Margolyes says: 'If you look like me, short, fat and Jewish, people really don't know what to do with you. Instead of using your peculiarities like they do in America, they don't know what to do with you here. They are frightened. There is too much of a cult of perfection.' Could this be another clue about the general fear and hatred of fat?

In a section on 'Looks, Glamour and the Image' in the same book, Eve Ferret is quoted as saying: 'Someone said to me, "Eve, when you first came on stage you reminded me of Bette Midler. But when I looked again you reminded me of Ronnie Barker."' Eve Ferret has sometimes been considered a latterday Diana Dors and has done a variety of film and television work. She also said: 'I don't fit into an ideal, but then I look at myself and I think "I feel quite normal".' She certainly celebrates her individuality and in *Absolute Beginners* she was inevitably cast as Big Jill because of her size, which she appreciates is part of her appeal. Capitalizing on her flamboyance, she refuses to change herself for any market and now directors are changing parts to suit her instead. She is glamorous, outrageous and big.

Hopefully in the 1980s we are seeing an attempt to break the stereotypes and to recognize large women for who they are rather than ridiculing them or using them in a particular way. Banks and Swift point out that in America there is less stereotyping and more chance for comic women to achieve their potential on film. This is not a reflection on the ability of the women on either side of the Atlantic but mostly, they suggest, to do with available funds. When funds flow readily, there is scope for experiment and imagination, but when they are low film-makers tend to stick to safe stereotyped roles and traditional stories. In other words, if male comedians or certain body images like fat ladies have worked well for the film moguls and backers in the past, then in times of tighter funding they will be used again. Thus large women have less chance of breaking the mould.

Referring specifically to familiar, predictable, male-dominated television sketch work, Eve Ferret says of the few parts available to women: 'It's rubbish. Rubbish. We're not well served. You have to make the best of a bad job.' But Bella Emberg is less critical of her material. She has played the large-lady stooge to many male comedians, including Benny Hill, Les Dawson, Frankie Howerd, Stanley Baxter and Russ Abbott, and says she is very happy playing second fiddle. 'I don't mind as long as it makes people laugh – that's the main thing. If it works, that's all that matters.'

I find that depressing. It is unfortunate to base your act on the defensive theory that if you laugh at your own size first, then perhaps people will laugh with you more than at you. It is another sad reinforcement of the stereotype that large is ridiculous. In a society where men are still dominant and women are treated as an inferior group, large women are considered even more subordinate and inferior and are therefore even more likely to be the butt of male jokes. So why make them the victims of female comedians too?

However, every now and then there is a gleam of hope for large actresses, even in straight drama. In Fay Weldon's story *The Life and Loves of a She-Devil*, the title role was proclaimed as a marvellous television part for a large woman since the actress was given a positive, straight role. But Julie T. Wallace found herself playing a physically unattractive woman with facial hair and a mole (presumably to enhance the unacceptability of large women in general). During the story she supposedly blossomed and in some of the scenes she wore beautiful clothes and looked very attractive, but unfortunately she did so not for herself but for the sake of someone else. Finally she suffered a major surgical ordeal in order to look exactly like her rival for her husband's affections. The whole story became one not about a large woman who was powerful and used her power appropriately but about a woman who desperately and unrealistically tried to be exactly like someone else – a petite woman – so that she could be loved. So what starts out as hope becomes yet again a disappointment.

The most positive television image that I can recall

for a large woman was in the *Bergerac* series. The character of a personal assistant played by Annette Badland was quite large. She was shown actually cycling to work – at last here was a large woman who was fit and active and had the kind of job in which the stereotype is usually glamorous and thin. As an actress, however, Badland has faced considerable discrimination because of her size.

In Nancy Roberts's book *Breaking All the Rules*, Badland reveals that she was once booked for a comedy show purely as a large tonnage of flesh to squash the star's transistor radio – a deeply humiliating role. She is clear-sighted about society's prejudices, well aware that people 'assume a particular character goes with size – either a depressed failure, someone who is terribly unhappy with themselves, or someone dominating.' However, she always seeks to make the most of her acting opportunities and, given a part because of her size, she then sets about finding different aspects in the role, developing the character so that her size becomes irrelevant.

To return to comedy, where large women find many more outlets, Victoria Wood is a highly talented performer and she deals well and humorously with the position of women in society without making them victims or denigrating them in any way. She is certainly 'above average' in size and she dresses beautifully, which I believe matters. Clothes do play an important part in many women's lives (remember how the She-devil's clothes expressed her new attractiveness?). For a large woman, however, the assumption remains that she is ashamed of her size and that she wants to look smaller, thinner, shorter – that overall she wants to shrink and not to draw attention to any part of her body by emphasizing it. Thus the ubiquitous tent came into being, the universal disguise, often with a little white bow under the neck and a Peter Pan collar. In theory the white tie draws the eye, not to a good face but to the least fat part of the body.

In *Breaking All the Rules*, there is a list of pitfalls in dressing that large women are supposed to avoid. For example, never wear horizontal stripes; stick to dark colours; avoid patterns and ruffles and belts; keep away from round necklines or short necklaces, heavily gathered sleeves, double-breasted jackets, broad-shouldered tops; don't wear large, round earrings or hoops, or billowy sleeves, bows or flounces; draw attention away from the waist by wearing fussy bits around the neckline; never wear satin, because it reflects light in all the wrong places, and never wear linen because it creases – and creases spell fat. Frankly, these rules make me angry. A large woman is an individual, like any other woman, and she should wear what feels and looks good for *her* rather than adhere to a set of someone else's rules.

The fashion world also dictates the large woman's choice by failing to make their normal ranges available above a certain size – sometimes 14 is the limit, sometimes 16. If they do extend the range, they charge more for the same style in larger sizes, claiming that more material is needed – which any dressmaker knows is nonsense. It is usually assumed that a woman of larger size will want to dress differently to disguise herself and no allowance seems to be made for the importance of proportion appropriate to the individual, which is the basis of good dress sense (see Chapter 7). Things are slowly changing: in the last couple of years a few manufacturers have introduced exciting ranges for larger women but they tend to produce them in small quantities and therefore at high prices.

I have asked manufacturers why they do not offer more choice by making their full range available in all sizes and been told that women would not buy them. Well, perhaps at first they would not. Large women have spent too many hours going from shop to shop and being told by a slim whippet of a sales assistant: 'We don't have anything in *your* size, madam.' (It is particularly insensitive to have skinny teenage assistants in departments which specialize in larger sizes.) Unless new styles and new policies towards large sizes are well advertised, disenchanted women will not have the heart to keep hunting, and if the prices remain artificially high, only a few will be able to afford them anyway.

There are a few special shops for larger women, of course, but their clothes tend to be imported, since the Americans and Europeans cater for large women rather better than the British designers and manufacturers, who equate large clothes with frumpiness and then insist on displaying them on small models, which destroys all the proportions anyway. Imported clothes are naturally more expensive and a typical wage-earner, or an unemployed woman or full-time housewife, can never scrape together enough money at one time to afford a £60 skirt or a £100 dress. Among the women I have met at my workshops, those who could scrape that sort of money together would be reluctant to spend it on themselves anyway: they would feel guilty.

Yet the magazine *Extra Special* (which, incidentally,

some newsagents offered in plain brown wrappers from under the counter as if it was pornography) found in its market research that nearly 50 per cent of British women wear clothes of size 16 or larger, and they come from every level of society. One wonders whether the clothes manufacturers' research has been as thorough and how much of an effort they have made to find out what large customers really want.

Finding a swimsuit, a tracksuit, sun-dresses, trousers, sportsgear, shorts, T-shirts – the clothes that most women buy for the summer – can be a nightmare for large women. At a time when there is an increasing emphasis on health and fitness, the clothes manufacturers should be encouraging large women to participate in such activities and should be producing attractive items for them to wear, but apart from one or two exclusive firms this does not appear to be the case. (Shops and mail-order firms specializing in larger sizes are listed in Appendix II.)

There is no reason why a large woman should not be fit and well exercised and, like any other woman, she would feel much better in herself for it. Yet even something as simple as an exercise bike is denied her, since most of them have weight limits which make it impossible for a large woman to use them.

Fitness and health are generally equated, but many people, even in the medical world, seem to be blind to the fact that a large woman can be fit. Health promotion organizations in some cities, for example, will not employ people over a certain weight because the authorities do not feel that large people can represent a 'healthy' image. The medical profession in general equates large size with lack of fitness and over-eating. Many large women have visited their doctor for a straightforward physical problem such as, say, a verruca or damaged finger, and have had their symptoms disregarded while the conversation focuses on their weight, however irrelevant it might be to the original medical condition. Some doctors will deny treatment until the woman loses weight, and not only are her real symptoms seen by the doctor as less important than her so-called weight problem but she is made to feel incapable of defining her own problems. An assertive way of dealing with visits to the doctor is suggested on pages 133–5.

One begins to wonder whose body it is, anyway. It must be accepted that severe obesity might increase the risk of complications under anaesthetics, or might in some cases make certain operations more awkward for the surgeon but many other physical conditions also complicate surgical procedures – such as asthma, old age, blood disorders and, ironically, underweight. The difference is in the attitude of the medical profession, who view most of the latter conditions sympathetically as being inflicted by circumstance and presenting management problems which the surgeon's team needs to cope with – challenges to be accepted, if you like. Obesity, however, is often criticized as a self-inflicted disability which the patient rather than the medical team ought to manage: the overweight patient is assumed to be not an innocent victim of circumstance but a guilty self-indulger.

Women also go to their GPs with emotional difficulties, and here again the doctor often automatically assumes that these are connected with weight. Of course, that may well be the case. Women who believe that they are fat come under considerable stress because of discrimination against their size, and the stress may lead to a loss of self-esteem, a sense of shame and feelings of guilt, which in turn lead to stringent dieting. But a rigorous, punitive diet regime starves the body (and depresses the mind) so that the body fights back and there is an overwhelming desire to binge wildly. That of course makes you feel fat again and also guilty about your indulgence, and you atone for it by dieting again, leading to further stress when that diet also fails – and so the carousel goes round and round as you get rounder. Depression and anxiety are emotions that are likely to break any dieter's resolve but dieting can itself cause anxiety, depression and apathy. The way to break this perpetual cycle is to love your body, not to fight it, and to win back your self-esteem.

THE DIETING CAROUSEL

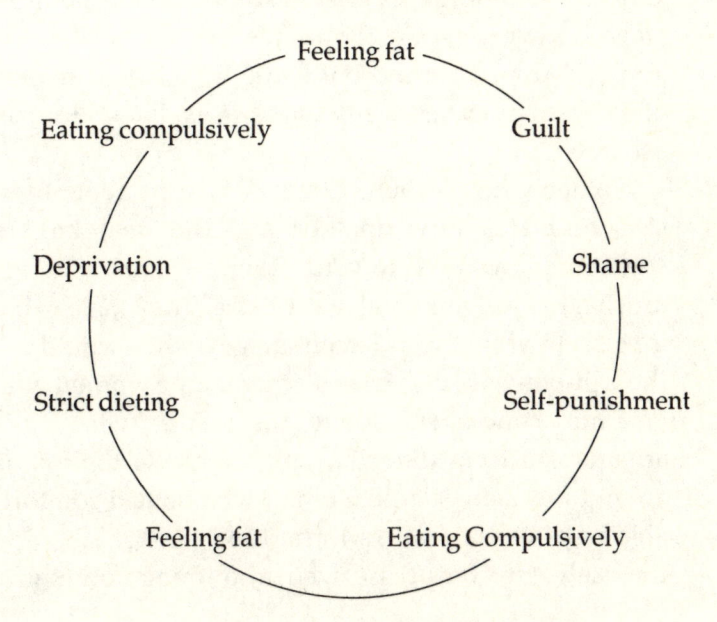

Feeling fat → Guilt → Shame → Self-punishment → Eating Compulsively → Feeling fat → Strict dieting → Deprivation → Eating compulsively → Feeling fat

The fashionable emphasis on health, well-being and fitness is in itself admirable but unfortunately it is very often equated with being slim. In other words, if you are large it is assumed you cannot be healthy or fit or feel good. Many of the so-called health clubs turn out to be slimming facilities and a large amount of money is made out of slimming aids, slimming exercises and various pills and potions which will supposedly help women to reduce their size and meet the 'ideal' image. There are hundreds of magazines and books, plenty of low-calorie food and drinks, calorie counters and much else.

There are also slimming clubs such as Weight Watchers where clients are given diet plans and a target weight which in my case I found unrealistically low. At the age of twenty-nine I was given a target which I had not even achieved at the age of twenty-one and size 14. The clubs work on the principle of giving or withholding praise. Each member is publicly weighed every week: if she has lost weight, she is applauded and praised but if she has gained there is of course no praise; instead she is likely to feel ashamed.

Women who are dieting or are unhappy about their size, no matter how small or large they may be, are sometimes punitive towards large women and are much more judgemental of their size. They have to be, in order to promote and maintain what they would call the will-power to continue dieting. Large women who are not concerned about their size will evoke antagonism from dieting women because their aims are not the same. Large women who do feel comfortable have refused to conform; they are not allowing themselves to be pressurized into doing something they feel is inappropriate or even damaging to them and to their bodies, and they are not actually going through the painful and distressing process of dieting. So it is little wonder that women who are dieting feel antagonistic towards them.

Guilt is not a good incentive: we can only change because we *want* to and because we love ourselves, not by punishing ourselves. In common with other therapists, I quite often find myself working with people who have failed at slimming clubs or clinics; sometimes they fail repeatedly and are effectively rejected by the clubs, sometimes they are encouraged to go back again and again because it is financially rewarding for the company. The therapists have to pick up the pieces of a shattered ego.

The *Observer* on 13 March 1988 investigated slimming clinics. Three journalists, none of whom was obese according to standard weight charts, visited different clinics. In every case they were prescribed something. One was given Duromine, an amphetamine appetite depressant for short-term use in the treatment of patients with moderate to severe obesity, and which should only be taken under close supervision as its side-effects may include insomnia, dry mouth, facial swelling, vomiting, rash, headache and possibly dependence or even mental illness. Another was given amino acids, which the medical profession claims are useless and a waste of time. The third was given Frusemide, a powerful diuretic which is normally prescribed for water retention due to heart or kidney failure; it causes the patient to pass copious amounts of urine and its side-effects include disturbances to the blood chemistry, low blood-pressure and fainting.

Each of the three journalist 'clients' had declared their intention of losing weight when they approached the clinics, and it is particularly disturbing that no counselling was given, despite the fact that it was obvious they did not need to slim. Any of them could have been anorexic. After a cursory interview, all were given drugs in unmarked containers and in no case was the medication prescribed by a qualified doctor. The drugs were either placebos or, as already described, diuretics or amphetamines which could have harmful side-effects. The article remarked: 'Clinics such as these, which prey on a rising number of people desperate to lose weight and prepared to pay well for it, are subject to no official checks or registration.'

As Egon Ronay put it in a *Sunday Times* article entitled 'Mrs Spratt, All is Forgiven': 'Facts are propounded without controlled laboratory tests. Diet madness is rampant; freaks have become the norm.'

Exposure of such clinics by papers like the *Observer* deserves every encouragement. The clinics obviously need monitoring, and those that issue any kind of drug should be under the strictest possible control by medical authorities. Those that are exposed as less than competent or scrupulous should be closed forthwith, and others should be registered and regularly inspected to ensure that the prescriptions they offer are suitable for the purpose for which they are used.

If all the women who believe themselves to be ugly, idle and greedy because of their size were able to see clearly that they are none of those things, a considerable number of exploitative industries would crash out of business. Too many fortunes are being made by those who profit from perpetuating the idea that slimness is desirable. Some of the measures that women will take to try and reduce their size are horrifically self-mutilating, and there are practitioners who are only too ready to carry out bizarre operations on women who seem to have been brainwashed by society into finding their bodies unacceptable. Very little seems to be done to help such women take a look at the issues involved and many surgical operations are condoned on the assumption that weight is a problem, without questioning whether it really is and without delving into the underlying causes of the woman's extreme and exaggerated dissatisfaction with her own body. Some of these appalling procedures are described in the next chapter.

3

IMAGES IN PERSPECTIVE

'Thin is beautiful' is a recent phenomenon, and by no means a universal one. By the late 1970s the winners of the Miss America beauty contest were on average an inch taller and five pounds lighter than their predecessors in the mid-1950s. Twiggy, the epitome of skinny models, weighed only 97 pounds at the peak of her career, and she was five feet seven inches tall.

Ironically, while the ideal image of the Western woman grew progressively thinner, in reality the average young woman's natural weight was increasing because of improved nutrition. It is little wonder that, according to a 1986 survey, three-quarters of American women believe they tend to be 'overweight' and that half of them are on diets 'most of the time'. There seems to be a touch of masochism in the way that fat oppression leads to diet obsession, even in the thin.

Susan Wooley, Associate Professor in the Psychiatry Department of the University of Cincinnati's College of Medicine, conducted that survey on behalf of *Glamour* magazine and found that 75 per cent of the 33,000 women who responded to her questionnaires said they were too fat, including 45 per cent who were actually *under*weight according to the 1959 Metropolitan Life Insurance Company's height and weight tables. (According to the revised tables issued in 1983, which set generally higher desirable weight levels, even more of the respondents would have been classified as underweight.)

Wooley, who was also co-director of the university's Eating Disorders Clinic and whose opinions are much respected, sees the contemporary obsession with weight as being partly a response to notions of 'equality'.

> This striving for thinness is to have a more masculine type body. As we join men's worlds we should not be cashing in women's bodies. We have to reclaim the right to have female bodies and still be respected. Thinness has become a cultural symbol of competency. If we buy that symbol and foster it ourselves, that is a very self-mutilating stand to take.

In the 1960s and 1970s Marabel Morgan and Helen Andelin were still writing books which advocated the subordination of women. Andelin's *Fascinating Womanhood* (1965) and Morgan's *Total Woman* (1973), which have sold millions of copies in the last two decades, are described in Rita Friedman's *Beauty Bound* as 'in essence cookbooks for cultivating signals of subordination'. For example, *Total Woman* suggests that if you are a large, tall or strong woman you should work to disguise these features so that men will see you as little and delicate.

No matter what your size, you can appear frail to men if you follow certain rules. It is not important that you actually be little and delicate but that you seem so to the man. Get rid of an air of strength, ability, competence or fearlessness and instead try to develop an air of frail dependency so that men will want to take care of you; and if you are efficient and capable in masculine things you will have to unlearn these trends.

We are all well aware of the reaction of today's women to such suggestions, but the new emancipation has perhaps developed too quickly for many people, especially men. The current trend in the United States is for top models to become younger, slimmer, flat-chested and narrow-hipped: they look prepubescent, even if in reality they are too old for the part. Some speculate that this is part of a backlash against the feminist movement and that men, threatened by women demanding their rights and a fairer deal in life, are retreating into fantasies of sexually immature women rather than 'real' women with breasts and child-bearing hips.

In *Beauty Bound*, Friedman describes the prepubertal models portrayed in fashion advertisements and fashion sketches as long-legged, lean, and like late-maturing fourteen-year-olds. Pre-adolescent girls are usually well aware of the advantage of being childishly pretty, delicate and slender, dainty-footed and fair of face, and the advertisements often show such childish traits – pink cheeks, pastel clothes, wide misty eyes. These child fantasy models pose innocently asleep, or curled up in a chair, or they play with soft, cuddly rabbits and kittens, or hug themselves or even suck something as if they were toddlers. The image is of an alluring, defenceless, dependent girl who needs a man's protection.

That image gives some men a feeling of power and self-esteem: they are more attracted by childlike women who need their fatherly protection than by large, mature, independent women who take up space and do not need to be looked after. Historically, woman has been passive and man active. Now that women have banded together and become more active themselves, which often means that they are tougher, stronger and more powerful, some men have found them threatening and are uncertain of their own role in society. They were much more comfortable when they performed the powerful, active role themselves and they want women to remain as the submissives men are more able to deal with.

The little-girl look is currently sexually alluring but it also conveys the neediness which such men find attractive. The commercial world has cottoned on to the fact that this particular prepubescent image will attract men who are finding the reality of coping with strong women difficult. In their fantasies, men believe (or the advertisements seek to imply) that the kittenish vamp wants only to please her father-figure, which is very different from a woman who is clear about her needs and asks directly for them – they find that threatening.

However, there is more to the thinness fashion than insecure men. It seems that, in the Western world at least, the image of the ideal woman shrinks in times of affluence and expands again when times are hard. One popular but inadequate explanation for this is that the affluent are slimmer because they eat more lean meat and vegetables while the poor fill up on starchy food, but this does not account for the fact that populations of poor males tend to have a lower percentage of fat individuals than non-poor males. In *Fat Phobia*, Nancy Worcester says that in England and North America obesity is more common in working-class women than in women of higher socio-economic groups but that with men the relationship between class and bodyweight is not so well defined. Both poor men and poor women have less access to healthy, non-fattening foods, so why the difference in their obesity?

Some may say that the size difference between men from different classes is because of the type of work men do and that the working-class man is likely to be employed in manual labour: he offsets any tendency to obesity by doing more physical labour than a middle-class man. This fails to take into account that the middle-class man has better access to leisure exercise facilities, nor does it explain why working-class women, who like their male counterparts are more likely to be involved in physically active jobs than middle-class women, have a greater tendency to obesity than the latter.

Nancy Worcester turns the whole question around by asking, 'Is it possible that, in our society, a woman's body build is a factor in *determining* her socio-economic status?' In 1968 S. J. Cahnman, in a paper entitled 'The Stigma of Obesity', concluded that 'obesity, especially as far as girls are concerned, is not so much a mark of socio-economic status as a condemnation of it.' In 1965 a study on *Social Factors in Obesity* looked at a sample of 1,600 adults in Manhattan and noted that overweight women were far less likely than non-obese women to achieve a higher socio-economic status than their parents; indeed they were more likely to have a lower status. However, this relationship was not found in men.

In 1966 Canning and Muir published a paper on 'Obesity – Its Possible Effects on College Acceptance', which found that non-obese women were more likely to be accepted in college than obese women, even though they did not differ in intellectual ability or in the percentage of each category applying for college education. Canning and Muir described the likely outcome of this discrimination: 'If obese adolescents have difficulty in attending college, substantial numbers experience a drop in social class or fail to advance beyond present levels. Education, occupation and income are social class variables that are strongly interrelated. A vicious circle therefore may begin as a result of college admission discrimination preventing the obese from rising in the social class system.'

All in all, then, it seems that much more influential than such simple economic matters as lean meat versus potatoes are factors like class, sex, race and tradition.

Weight and wealth have long been associated. The Duchess of Windsor is quoted in *Beauty Bound* as saying: 'You cannot be too thin or too rich.' Many women, especially Americans, seem to have taken her gospel to heart. Trends tend to filter down from those who have, petering out as they reach the have-nots. The sociologist Thorstein Veblen (died 1929) noted that body shape reflected conspicuous consumption and that curves signified luxury. When resources are scarce, weight is associated with prosperity and plump women are admired. Indeed, in the ancient oriental view, a well-fed woman brought honour to her husband, and in other cultures powerful chieftains sometimes force-fed their women as a testimony to their own wealth. But when resources are plentiful the weight caste system is reversed: the rich can afford to be thin because they have the choice of eating as little or as much as they like.

In the United States today obesity is seven times more common among women of lower socio-economic levels than those in higher income brackets (though among men the social-class differences in weight remain minimal); conversely, anorexia is rare among lower-class families but is increasing among upper-class women. Somehow thinness is seen to conform with the American values of hard work and self-denial: being thin is virtuous and a sign of economic success, while overweight is shamefully lower class. Thus fat represents low social status and lack of self-control.

In Britain class and regional factors seem to play a part. I come from Coventry and now live in the south: in common with many other migrants, I feel like a freak in the south but become more acceptable the further north I travel. This seems to reflect the north–south wealth division so beloved of the media. There is also a racial element: it is much more acceptable for a woman to be large if she is, say, of West Indian origin, and some of the most positive role models for large women are black and proud of their size.

There is also a theory that, with the world generally attempting to limit population growth on this crowded planet, pregnancy is becoming less important and that, as women become less immersed in motherhood, slimness (the obvious opposite of the pregnant figure) symbolizes emancipation.

All this may be true in, say, Britain, North America and Australasia, but in many other parts of the world the trend to thinness is resisted. In many Mediterranean countries, for example, large women are still seen as assets. There is a recognized connection between a woman's large 'child-bearing' hips and generous bust and her fertility. Fertility is still important in regions where it is advantageous to have many children. A large wife can also be seen as a social asset, of value to a man's status because she demonstrates that he is able to support, feed and care for her. When I visit a country like Turkey I am considered attractive and I enjoy the admiration of the men, so different from the disapproving stares which too often come my way in Britain. A holiday in Turkey can be highly recommended as an ego-booster for large women!

Twenty-five thousand years ago, in palaeolithic times, fat was clearly commendable. Venus figurines have been found in regions stretching from Spain to Eurasia, representing full-bodied women with big breasts, swollen abdomens, huge thighs and large, round bottoms. Some archaeologists suggest that the figures were goddesses who embodied men's awe of women's reproductive powers and who were worshipped at times when famine was a way of life and fertility was a mystery.

The slim, diminutive models of today might have been as oppressed in those ancient cultures as large women so often are in our own culture. Indeed, as recently as the seventeenth century, for example, any woman in Holland who weighed less than about seven stone was suspected of being a witch; after all, it was argued, she was deemed to be light enough to ride on a broomstick. There is still a pair of witches' scales in Oudewater, a village near Rotterdam, on which suspiciously thin women from all over the country were weighed. Those unable to tip the scales were thrown into the canal with their hands tied to test the theory that innocent women would float but witches would sink. Luckily for large women, they do in fact tend to float more readily than thin ones!

The Greeks, according to Rita Friedman in *Beauty Bound*, envied the Cretans for a mysterious drug which kept them thin, while the Romans, 'who hated obesity but also loved to feast, used regurgitation to keep the scale figures down'. Does that remind you of our own society?

Marcia Millman, writing in 1980, looks at the situation in the Western world in more recent times. 'Between 1400 and 1700 the maternal role was idolized and fat was considered fashionable and erotic. Wives were chosen for their ability to have babies and spent much of their lives either pregnant or nursing. The ideal image of beauty portrayed matronly plumpness and the fruitful look of a Botticelli nymph.' In 1702 Queen Anne came to the British throne, and in no time at all fashionable women were doing everything they could to be plump and display a double chin just like the queen. By the late 19th century women were padding out inadequate figures by wearing bustles to broaden their bottoms: even their doctors encouraged the buxom look as a sign of good health. Millman draws attention to mammoth sculptures like the Statue of Liberty in which an admirable woman is big-boned, solid and sensually rounded.

Images in Perspective

One only has to stroll around an art gallery to see how women's shapes have changed. The Rubens woman, for example, is large in bust and hip, and although she has a figure-of-eight shape her waist is not particularly narrow and she is well covered with flesh. Voluptuous women were also painted by Renoir, for example in 'The Seated Bather Drying Her Leg'. Rodin's statues in the Tuileries and in his museum in Paris are large, full-breasted, full-hipped women; Henry Moore's figures are women of substance; and there are many other examples of large women being appreciated by painters and sculptors. Edwardian 'naughty' pin-up postcards were always of large, well-rounded women, usually dressed in body stockings and holding bits of lace and bowls of fruit; they all look as if they weighed a good eleven stone and were at least a size 18.

Every society in every age has its own concepts of beauty in women and, encouraged by their mothers and peers, women often go to extreme lengths to mould their bodies to fit that desirable image. Fashions for small waists, for example, have led women in different periods to wear a variety of corsets and stays, very often so restricting the capacity of their lungs that they were unable to take in adequate oxygen or to eat properly. Hence, not surprisingly, they had a tendency to faint, and the frail, swooning beauty was in reality quite ill.

This practice was still in vogue to some extent quite recently. I well remember being one of a team of three women trying to lace another woman into her corsets, pushing a foot or knee into her back in order to tighten the stays as much as possible. That was only forty years ago. However, it was nothing like as drastic as the surgical removal of two lower ribs which was some Edwardian women's answer to the desire for a tiny waist. Considering how life-threatening surgery can still be today, the risks of such operations in those days are even more horrifying.

In the 1920s flat chests were very much in vogue and many women took to bust-binding, which entailed wrapping a long, broad piece of material as tightly as possible around the bosom to flatten it. Any woman will recognize how painful that must have been. In more recent times, breast size has been reduced by cosmetic surgery, or enlarged by silicone implants.

To take an extreme example of reducing a woman physically in order to make her more 'attractive', in China mothers of a certain social class would bind their baby daughters' feet, crippling the children so that they could hardly walk and they grew into ornaments rather than useful, active women. A Chinese husband betrayed one of the major psychological benefits of this practice – from the man's point of view.

> My memory is not strong; I cut a poor figure; I am timid and my voice is not strong among men. But to my footbound wife, confined for life to our house except when I bear her in my arms, my stride is firm, my voice is that of a roaring lion, my wisdom is that of the sages. To her I am the world: I am life itself.

Rita Friedman, quoting this statement in *Beauty Bound*, remarks that clearly the acknowledged purpose of footbinding was to prevent a woman's freedom to wander, and thus give her husband control over her and a feeling that he was firm and powerful. But why did the mothers pander so blatantly to the male ego? Friedman quotes one mutilated woman as saying:

> My mother didn't feel bad about the pain suffered when binding my feet because if a girl was plain-looking but had small feet, she might still be considered a beauty, but if she had large feet, no matter how good-looking she might be, no one would marry her.

(Shades of Cinderella's 'Ugly Sisters' trying to cram their feet into the glass slipper!)

A good marriage, with all the potential for prosperity and status which it confers, was also the motivation for the mutilating practice of female circumcision (often clitoridectomy) in certain African and Islamic cultures. The physical removal of the clitoris in young women was still quite a common practice in the 1970s, especially in rural areas. The Egyptian feminist Nawal El Saadawi, interviewed in *Spare Rib* in 1979, pointed out that it was a remnant of the chastity belt: the aim was to diminish female sexuality for the sake of monogamous marriage in a patriarchal society. The practice was a major item on the 1979 agenda of a World Health Organization seminar on traditional health practices, held in Khartoum, when representatives of seven countries recommended that it be abolished.

However, only a couple of years ago there was an outcry in London about young girls being circumcised in private British clinics. It was found that such operations were still encouraged by women of particular cultural groups because no uncircumcised young woman would be acceptable as a bride, and the only way a woman could survive was to be married. Therefore the custom was perpetuated by the women themselves despite the acknowledged cruelty, pain and outrage inflicted upon young girls by the operation, which left them mutilated and psychologically damaged. And it was happening right here in Britain. A custom we had shrugged off as being that of far-away tribal peoples living in some unimaginable Dark Age suddenly thrust itself into the midst of our own society. Our memories are short, however, because in the 19th century a British doctor, Baker Brown, had set quite a fashion for the operation as a cure for 'hysteria'. He claimed that an autonomous sexual drive led to every form of rebellion and 'moral leprosy' in a woman. As recently as 1953 a twelve-year-old girl in Kentucky had been the victim of clitoridectomy.

The point of what might seem like a diversion from the main themes of this book is that these mutilations were encouraged by women – mothers – because they believed that otherwise their daughters would not be marriageable, and that without a good marriage they would not be able to progress well in life. In our culture today, mothers still mould their daughters for the same reason, but not on the whole with such drastic methods. They teach little girls to be pretty, which means to conform to the ideal lean shape. By encouraging them to diet and to wear clothes which make them appear slimmer, they imply that there is something wrong with their daughters' natural shape. Little wonder they become self-conscious about their own bodies.

Images in Perspective

In *Beauty Bound*, Friedman points out that women of college age are very aware of their breasts and some are so embarrassed by these very obvious signs of femininity that they are tempted into the irreversible remedy of breast reduction surgery. Until only relatively recently, such surgery was not performed on minors because it was bound to lead to regrets later in life. However, one plastic surgeon notes that parents often now initiate a request for surgery, and he cautions doctors to make sure that the girl herself really wants the operation and also understands the pain and potential consequences. Complications are common with reduction mammoplasty, including unsightly scarring and loss of nipple sensitivity. The surgeon asks whether it is possible for an emotionally immature girl, who has a poor body image and who is probably suffering from ridicule, to make a wise decision about something as drastic as cosmetic breast surgery.

Because breasts are so symbolic of the feminine body in Western cultures, many physically normal girls experience almost paralysing selfconsciousness during the natural maturation process. Full-breasted girls, especially those who mature early, are embarrassed and overtly ridiculed, and there is a strong tendency for large-breasted women of any age to be labelled as 'unintelligent, incompetent, immoral and immodest' (as Isak Dinesen once said). In the present climate of thin ideal images and the use of immature models in fashion, no wonder the budding adolescent sometimes resents her breasts. But that is no excuse for parents to encourage uninformed and dependent young women to undergo some physical and irreversible adaptation of their bodies in order to be 'acceptable' or perhaps 'marriageable'.

In the same name of beauty, all sorts of horrific operations are carried out today on women of all ages by private cosmetic surgeons. No one really knows how many suffer unnecessary surgery or how often it causes more harm than good. Fortunes can be made out of the vanity of women, or rather out of their desperation at not conforming naturally to the ideal image and being unable to bear the consequent oppression. In too many cases, surgeons fail to examine the underlying causes of their patients' dissatisfaction; they blithely agree with the woman who believes that fat is bad, and offer to help her get rid of what she sees as excess weight without discussing the many other issues that surround what she perceives as her problem. It is a little like putting rouge on the cheeks of a severely anaemic patient instead of diagnosing and curing the cause of the anaemia.

Jaw-wiring is one of the procedures which is offered to women who are considered grossly obese. The teeth (rather than the jaw) are wired together so that it is impossible to chew and the only nutritional intake is in the form of liquids. A recent article in *Prima* magazine ('Weird but not so wonderful ways to lose weight') gave the case of a woman from north London who had been overweight for twenty years. Weighing 21 stone and desperate to reduce her size, she decided to have her jaws wired. 'I went mad for the first few days,' she said, 'because I desperately wanted to eat solids. But after that it wasn't too bad. I was on 800 calories a day and I lost five stone in three or four months.' When her weight had been reduced to 15 stone, her specialist decided to have the wires removed. She goes on to say: 'Gradually, I began to eat more . . . and more . . . and instead of losing any more weight, it began to creep up again. Now, sadly, I'm even heavier than I was before I was wired. At the end of the day it's all down to you. There is no real substitute for will-power.'

At the Clinical Research Centre at Harrow, Middlesex, a study was made (by J. S. Garrow and G. T. Gardiner) of a group of patients whose weight loss was maintained after their jaws were freed because a nylon cord had been fastened around their waists as a psychological barrier to weight gain. Seven patients followed up for 4–14 months after removal of jaw-wiring regained a mean of only 5.6kg of the 31.8kg they had lost which, the researchers claimed, compared favourably with other treatments for severe obesity. But what happened after that? Research at the Eastern General Hospital in Edinburgh in 1986 showed that a high percentage of people who have their jaws wired put all the weight back on again within a year or two.

Jaw-wiring is not surgical in that the skin is not broken, but it is carried out under local anaesthetic at a hospital by a dental surgeon who cements the wire in place. The major types of weight-loss surgery are even more drastic. One is the intestinal or jejunoileal bypass (*jejunus* is the Latin for 'hungry', and the jejunum is part of the small intestine between the duodenum and the ileum) which involves disconnecting most of the small intestine. It has been carried out since the 1950s, but it has now generally been replaced by the new gastric or 'stomach stapling' procedures (gastric bypass, gastroplasty and gastric partitioning). The first gastric bypass for weight loss was performed in 1966 and it involves separating a 2oz portion of the stomach, then reconnecting the intestines to that small portion so that the rest of the stomach is bypassed. In gastroplasty a 12mm hole is left at the end of a row of staples near the greater curvature of the stomach. With gastric partitioning, the hole is located in the middle of the row. Both these stomach stapling procedures allow the food to pass through the entire stomach but at a much slower rate than normal.

None of these procedures has been standardized so far and their advantages or disadvantages have not yet been clearly established. They are experimental in that no long-term (20–30 years) study is yet available, and very few short-term ones. Nor is anyone at all certain that permanent weight loss can be achieved by these methods.

Yet in the United States thousands of obese women have submitted to such operations. As Susan Wooley and her husband Dr Orland Wooley point out: 'If a totally effective anti-obesity drug was discovered today, it would be many years before it would be available to the public. And if its mortality and morbidity risks were comparable to those of gastric and intestinal bypass, it seems doubtful that its use would ever be approved.'

One of the criteria for patient selection for these operations is morbid obesity, which is defined as either 100 pounds 'overweight' or, more commonly, at least double the 'ideal' weights defined by Metropolitan Life Insurance charts. There are cases where people are deemed to be so unhealthy that the benefits of the operation are assumed to outweigh the risks, but such cases are rare and the operation is all too frequently performed primarily for cosmetic reasons. In other words, women risk their health and perhaps their lives in the effort to conform to society's ideal shape.

Such radical surgical intervention is generally justified by the claim that 'morbidly obese patients have a mortality rate ten times that of non-obese patients'. Even if we accept these statistics, the assumption that losing weight will restore the obese patient's longevity to normal is unproven. The Wooleys, discussing surgical treatments, say: 'There is no evidence that their use increases longevity; in fact, the reverse may be true.' According to the *American Surgeon* (August 1978), mortality rates for intestinal bypasses ranged from 1 to 15 per cent with an average of 4 per cent, and those for gastric procedure ranged in most reports from 1 to 5 per cent with a 3–4 per cent average – one apparently considered acceptable by many surgeons. Surely such a risk cannot be acceptable for cosmetic reasons?

As Dr Labhart put it in the *South African Medical Journal*: 'Too often an intestinal bypass operation converts a healthy fat person into a sickly thin person.' When you consider that these operations are ostensibly performed to improve health, it is alarming to learn how many side-effects are considered a normal part of the procedure. They include malnutrition, diarrhoea, liver damage and kidney failure for intestinal bypasses; and nausea, vomiting, hernias, stomach perforation and spleen injury for gastric operations. Frequently the side-effects put the patient back into hospital for additional surgery to revise or reverse the original procedure, and as many as 25 per cent of intestinal bypass patients have had their operations reversed. Louise Wolf, who has done considerable research into weight-loss operations, is the author of 'Weight Loss Surgery: Miracle Cure or Mutilation?' published in the book *Shadow on a Tightrope* (1983). She says that, to her knowledge, no American states have compared health and longevity of surgical weight-loss patients with fat people who choose traditional treatment or no treatment at all; and this information is needed in order to evaluate the surgery adequately.

Considering that surgery is generally deemed to be more hazardous when performed on obese people, it is ironic that there has been such a rush towards weight-loss surgery in recent years. The National Institutes of Health conference in America in 1978, discussing surgical treatment and morbid obesity, said: 'Patients should receive a thorough explanation about the risks, benefits and uncertainties of each bypass procedure and be programmed to choose between them.' Note that the option of choosing *no* procedure is not even mentioned and one cannot help but wonder whether the doctors, in America anyway, are truly impartial in their advice. After all, there is perhaps $6000 in hospital revenue at stake for each operation, and numerous studies have shown that the medical profession tends to be biased against fat people anyway. To be fair, however, another report found that 95 per cent of intestinal bypass patients 'purposely denied the truth about past medical and social problems' (both patient and doctor are influenced by anti-fat prejudices) and this made informed consent almost impossible. The *American Journal of Nursing* once explained that a patient may also 'not hear the explanations of risk' because they want the operation and perceive only the facts that support their decision. I would agree with that.

In the *Prima* article referred to earlier, the story of the jaw-wired patient is followed by those of the drastic measures taken by four other women who wanted to lose weight. A Berkshire woman who had doubled her weight to 18 stone by her late forties was advised by a specialist that her heart muscles were being worn out by the extra burden and, after careful consultation, including advice about possible side-effects and the drastic nature of the operation, she agreed to undergo gastroplasty. She said that the operation was extremely painful but that she lost four stone in four months and is now ten stone four, a weight with which she is happy. 'I can get into a size 14 now. More important, my heart is fine. For all the problems, I'd have my stomach stapled all over again. The world looks down on fat people, and I hated that prejudice. Now I'm just enjoying being one of the crowd.'

One thing which alarms me about this article is that the possibility of long-term side-effects from stomach stapling is mentioned but no details are given. What concerns me even more is that, despite references to her health, the emphasis of this woman's remarks is on the prejudice of society. Are we in fact to go through such painful and dangerous procedures simply to conform?

The other *Prima* women had tried acupuncture, hypnotherapy and the intragastric balloon. This balloon, which is about the size of a hand, is implanted in the stomach and then inflated. Like stomach stapling, its effect is to reduce the size of the stomach, but it is not permanent. It can be deflated and withdrawn through the mouth or bowels. A clinical trial was conducted in 1987 by Dr Vincent Taylor, who found that on average obese patients lost two pounds a week while the balloon was in place, but the procedure is not generally available in the UK. It sounds rather less gruesome than the practice of well-to-do ladies in pre-Victorian times who occasionally had live tapeworms implanted in their stomachs to eat the food before it turned to fat, so that the women could indulge themselves without putting on pounds.

Finally, the *Prima* article described four ways of boosting will-power to cut down on eating – methods which are painless and cheap or cost-free. It suggests drinking half a pint of water before every meal to feel more full, or tying a piece of cord tightly round the waist, permanently, so that it becomes uncomfortable when you eat too much (the trick used by women who have had jaw-wiring removed), or plastering on a face-mask whenever you feel that urge to eat (imagine that in a restaurant!), or sticking a picture of your fat self on the fridge door next to one of a lean lady. That last idea in particular relies on self-disgust. I believe that we can only change something fundamental about ourselves through love and kindness, not through guilt. Anyway, who says we must all be thin?

So any of the more outrageous surgical assaults on the 'obese' body are carried out for the good of the patient's health, or so it is claimed. But is it not possible that body fat can be beneficial? For example, it gives a woman bodily reserves which can see her through times of famine and illness. Before such medicines as antibiotics were available, it was often a matter of having to live through a crisis during the course of an illness and survival depended on body reserves. Larger women would have survived more readily than thin women, so that large would have been seen as healthy as well as delectable. Those were the days!

4

THE MYTHS EXPOSED

Faced with a lifelong barrage of criticism, whether openly expressed or more subtly implied, it is little wonder that large women begin to do battle with their bodies even while they are still young girls. A large woman often feels that it is impossible for her to look good; she believes that she will remain unacceptable until she becomes smaller, and therefore she finds it difficult to be kind to her own despised body, to take good care of it, to keep fit and dress well or generally to accept her body, feel comfortable with it and good about herself.

Some women, who seem to have achieved the 'ideal' size, might become obsessed with the amount and type of food they eat in order to maintain that size, yet even those closest to them can be quite unaware of the enormous amount of time and energy they waste every day in the battle with their bodies.

Advertising is designed both to keep food on the mind of the consumer, making her aware of her appetite, and to influence her choice of products.

Dieting works in much the same way in that while we are dieting we are constantly concerned about how much we eat, and food is uppermost in our minds. Thus, paradoxically, at a time when we are consciously attempting to limit our food intake we are most likely to be aware of food. Most people have had the experience of missing lunch because they were concentrating so hard on the job in hand. No one on a diet is likely to be unaware of meal-times!

It used to be claimed that the difference between fat people and thin people was that the former ate according to information from outside like set meal-times, attractive food and social situations, whereas thin people ate in response to bodily information like hunger signals; this implied that thin people were less likely to eat more than their bodies needed. These ideas are now being revised. William Bennett and Joel Gurin, in *The Dieter's Dilemma*, suggest that, yes, people do respond to internal and external cues; someone on a diet will of course respond to external cues because food is so important while they are measuring and counting and carefully selecting what they eat. But dieting also creates a state of almost constant hunger, so there is no way a dieter can respond to internal cues without breaking the diet and eating almost continuously to satisfy her body's needs.

Dieting is a dangerous game. Senior psychologist Dr John Blundell, of Leeds University, reported to a meeting of the British Psychological Society in April 1988 that physiological changes occur during dieting which include alterations in the balance of neurochemicals. 'Dieting is a powerful assault on the body,' he explained, 'and the body responds by protecting itself. Metabolism slows down to expend less energy, and changes can even be measured in the brain.' Fat is less metabolically active than muscle, so the greater the proportion of fat that a body carries, the lower the overall metabolic rate of the body and the less energy it requires from food. Thus every diet effectively trains the body to become less energetic, requiring less energy from food and using less energy and oxygen with which to burn food. Habitual dieters are on a downward spiral which remorselessly reduces their vitality, according to Geoffrey Cannon and Hetty Einzig in their book *Dieting Makes You Fat*. Blundell also claims that dieting is often self-defeating and could in some cases lead not only to unhappiness and frustration but also to mental illness.

Many women who put themselves on punitive, near-starvation diets do indeed find the whole business self-defeating, and that such regimes often produce irritating or harmful side-effects. For a start, outward appearance can be adversely affected. Although weight loss is often equated with beauty, dieting can reduce the elasticity of the skin (especially where weight is alternately lost and gained) and a substantial weight loss may leave tell-tale stretch-marks like those experienced by some women after pregnancy. Hair loss can be another problem: many diets are deficient in protein and after five to ten weeks the scalp begins to shed hair quite profusely.

Even a high-protein weight-loss diet will reduce the body's muscle tissue. Weight lost during the first week of such a diet is half water, a quarter fat and a quarter lean tissue. We can grow new bone cells or blood cells but once a muscle cell is lost it has gone for ever. Of course, a rapid five-pound loss does not mean two-

and-a-half pounds of dead muscle tissue: the protein is simply withdrawn from the cells. However, a proportion of the muscle cells do die and when that five pounds is regained, there is a higher ratio of fat to lean tissue. The more you diet, therefore, the fatter and weaker you become.

The sedentary dieter has even more problems. The body of a sedentary person used to fat will tend to regain fat and rebuild less muscle simply because muscle is used inadequately by an inactive person. When weight is regained after a diet, the body composition of a sedentary person alters: the proportion of lean tissue decreases, the proportion of fatty tissue increases. Muscle is lost and fat is gained.

Dieting leads to changes in behaviour, with both physical and emotional effects. Our bodies are geared to maintain a certain weight, the level of which is different for each individual. The control mechanism of this 'set point' is the hypothalamus, a vital one-inch part of both the nervous system and the endocrine glandular systems which secrete hormones into the bloodstream. Hormones are in effect chemical messengers which control a wide range of body functions and are essential to health, especially in relation to slower, long-term processes like growth and sexual development.

The hypothalamus is the point at which the nervous system and the endocrine system meet. Lying at the base of the brain close to the pituitary gland, it acts both as a receiver of messages (from the brain and from the hormone concentration in the blood) and as a co-ordinator controlling instinctive behaviour and body activity. For example, it includes centres which affect sleep, thirst, appetite, body temperature, water balance and sexual functions. It manufactures hormones, which are then stored and released by the pituitary gland.

The pituitary gland is directly connected to the hypothalamus by a stalk and lies immediately beneath it. The hormones it releases include those which affect the functions of the kidneys, the uterus, the ovaries and testes, the thyroid and adrenal glands, the secretion of milk, the increasing height of the body during childhood, and the balance of energy and tissue repair throughout life. It is not surprising, therefore, that the 'health' of the pituitary and, even more crucially, of the hypothalamus, are vital to the well-being of the body. Listen to your body, and treat your instincts with respect: the hypothalamus is doing its best to maintain a balance in your systems and to keep you healthy and alive.

Because the hypothalamus controls so many of the body's instinctive and automatic functions, any change in it can have far-reaching effects on the body; for example, causing extreme hunger triggering off uncontrollable eating, or temperature control failure leading to hypothermia or high fever, or sleep disorders like narcolepsy (sudden overwhelming sleepiness), or menstrual disorders including delayed or very early puberty and cessation or irregularity of menstrual periods. Changes in the activity of the hypothalamus are sometimes caused by inflammation, injury or tumours but more often by less obvious factors which do not actually cause structural damage to the organ itself.

In the context of dieting, the hypothalamus monitors the bloodflow constantly, working rather like a thermostat. When the blood's sugar level drops, the hypothalamus signals the brain to find food and eat it to restore the balance. During dieting, the hypothalamus may begin to assume that there is no food in the environment and that there is therefore little point in wasting the body's energy seeking it. Concentration becomes difficult and those on diets can tire quickly, suffer from insomnia and lose enthusiasm for physical activity and sex.

It is now thought that the set point for which our bodies are programmed is genetically determined. A recent study by Dr Albert J. Stunkard of the University of Pennsylvania found that the weight of adopted children correlated with that of their biological parents rather than their adoptive ones, which suggests that weight is controlled by genetics rather than by learned habits. But this does not mean that the set point cannot be changed.

Smoking, for example, lowers the set point by a few pounds. Ruth Priest, in a *Radiance* article ('10 Reasons not to Diet') pointed out that women have been encouraged to use cigarettes as a means of weight control for years – certainly since 1928 when the American Tobacco Company introduced the slogan, 'Reach for a Lucky instead of a sweet'. Because smoking affects the metabolic rate, some people do gain weight when they give up cigarettes and fear of weight gain is a major reason why women are often less successful than men in stopping the habit. Lung cancer has now overtaken breast cancer as the leading cause of death in middle-aged women in the United States (1986 Cancer Facts and Figures, published by the American Cancer Society). It would appear that some women are paying with their lives for the sake of weighing a few pounds less.

In contrast to smoking, dieting tends to raise the set point. Professor Susan Wooley says that a loss of five pounds virtually ensures a gain of six, which means that those who diet many times may well weigh far more than if they had never dieted at all. Dieting simply does not work and most diet studies put the failure rate at between 96 and 98 per cent.

Susie Orbach claims that in the long term 95 per cent of all dieters regain all the weight lost on diet regimes; it is certainly safe to say that the eventual result of dieting is as likely to be a net weight gain as a net weight loss. The Royal College of Physicians' report on obesity states: 'Maintenance of weight loss beyond one year was less satisfactory and all longer term studies have found that weight increases again in the majority of patients. In the most complete study, 154 of the 190 patients who had been treated one to five years previously were found for questioning. 25 (that is 16%) had maintained a weight loss of over 40 pounds and 27 (that is 17%) were heavier than at the start of the study.'

Those who do manage to keep the pounds off are people who make a career out of weight control, such as those whose livelihood may depend upon being acceptably thin. But very few people eat sparingly just after coming off a diet and almost invariably they respond to the body's craving by eating at least as much as they did before dieting. This is not through greed, stupidity or thoughtlessness but because the body needs energy and regeneration and it responds with signals of extreme hunger in the first days after a diet has ended.

A letter to the British medical journal *The Lancet* told of a twenty-three-year-old model who dieted to keep her job. Eventually, her hunger ran out of control and she sat down to a gargantuan meal of 'liver, kidneys, steak, eggs, cheese, bread, mushrooms, carrots, a whole cauliflower, ten peaches, four pears, two apples, four bananas, two pounds of plums, two pounds of grapes and two glasses of milk.' In theory this was a well-balanced assortment which contained all the vitamins, minerals and calories her starved body demanded, but the volume of food, consumed all in one sitting, was ludicrously gross. She gained nineteen pounds and then, like the old woman who swallowed a fly, she died.

This desire to gorge is one of the most serious effects of dieting. If we listen to our bodies, then when we have eaten enough the hypothalamus notes the higher blood sugar levels and signals the brain to stop eating. However, if the body's weight is below its set point, the signal is not sent: the stomach may be full but the cells are far from satisfied and the impulse to continue eating remains. While binges are not usually fatal, they can cause physical discomfort like extreme intestinal cramps and diarrhoea and can also produce deep emotional distress because the binger feels wildly out of control. A study carried out at Cornell University found that 68.1 per cent of its women students had binged at some time and 20 per cent considered themselves habitual binge eaters. Could it be that bingeing is common because dieting is so common? An understanding of cause must always precede the cure: once it is known *why* a person gorges, then the compulsion can be dealt with successfully.

Bingeing usually generates a feeling of self-disgust and some people compensate for gorging by taking laxatives and diuretics or resorting to self-induced vomiting. Health disorders and even fatalities due to bingeing and purging are increasing. Laxatives and diuretics can lead to dehydration, loss of essential salts, and a decrease in blood volume which can result in weak muscles, fever, a weak and rapid pulse, a very unpleasant sensation of threatening doom, and eventually a fatal drop in blood-pressure levels. Self-induced vomiting can result in potassium deficiency (which can be fatal), urinary infection, kidney failure, swollen salivary glands, tooth decay, muscular cramps, heart muscle cramps, depression, epileptic fits, cessation of menstruation, and infertility. Purging is clearly dangerous but many women persist with it, partly to punish themselves and partly because it is one of the few methods of weight control that seems to work. Those who regurgitate their food stay thin because the food has no chance of being absorbed through the intestinal wall. Thus the food cannot make you fat, but neither can it keep you fit and healthy.

The hypothalamus cannot be fooled. We can stuff ourselves with diet grapefruit until our stomachs are swollen and sore but we can still feel hungry. This is because when we start burning reserves of fat we produce various side products, including free fatty acids. When the hypothalamus detects these in the bloodstream, it directs the brain to eat because the exploitation of fat stores indicates starvation. At the same time it signals the body to conserve its energy, and during dieting these almost conflicting signals increase in direct proportion to the length and severity of the regime, with noticeable effects on both physical and emotional well-being. Large weight losses apparently reduce the activity of the catecholamine neurotransmitters which bridge the gap between nerve cells in the brain and are involved in the control of voluntary movement, emotional arousal, learning and memory. Hence the lack of concentration and general physical lassitude which so often affect dieters.

The only way to stop the instinctive signals from the hypothalamus to find food and save energy is to stop burning fat, and that can only be done by eating something 'forbidden' on a diet. Sooner or later nearly all of us must yield to the impulse to eat and there is no diet regime that can honestly promise you will lose weight without feeling hungry. Gadgets like plastic balloons inflated in the stomach are no more effective than stuffing your stomach with grapefruit. The body needs feeding, even if the stomach does not.

Even slow-loss diets do not work permanently but need to be repeated. If you achieve a certain weight on such a diet, then you need to monitor yourself and will have to continue to diet for short periods in order to maintain that weight. This is once again because your body interprets not satisfying its hunger over a period of several days as starvation and it responds by conserving energy and using calories sparingly. Every regular dieter knows about that infamous plateau at which, in spite of stringent dieting, there is little or no reduction in weight. By dieting you are threatening your own body and it does not intend to die: in fact it is fighting for survival, and you are the enemy.

Very few long-term and follow-up studies are carried out by organizations that promote slimming products or methods, including slimming clubs. I believe the reason is that diet regimes do not work and that the people responsible for the administration of diet regimes are often unwilling to admit to themselves, and certainly to overweight people, that the treatments will almost invariably fail in the long run. Like football pools promoters, they advertise only their rare winners.

The punitive diet regimes promoted by many of those in the slimming industry are based on guilt. The assumption is that large women eat more than their bodies actually need, which means that they are greedy. An enormous number of women feel guilty about their eating habits, and guilt soon leads to lack of self-esteem and a sense of isolation: they feel that if dieting to become slim does work, then there must be something terribly wrong with them if they fail. They begin to feel ostracized; they do not talk about their feelings or their size and they believe society is right to condemn them. This is the 'victim syndrome'. If we believe we are victims, we often feel powerless and then behave in a powerless fashion. It is all too easy to shrug and say, 'What's the use? What is the point of all the self-denial, the depression?' The victim does nothing, feeling that she is not worthy enough to challenge what is happening to her. She becomes secretive about how she feels and begins to conform with her oppressors' opinion of her, accepting their judgement and blaming herself.

This sense of isolation and lack of self-esteem is common among the women who join our Big and Beautiful workshops, and our first task is to build up self-confidence. They are often surprised to hear about the disadvantages of dieting described in this chapter, and even more surprised to learn about some of the advantages of being large. There are certainly some health risks associated with being grossly overweight – including an increased risk of uterine cancer, high blood-pressure and diabetes – but an *improved* diet (as opposed to a reducing diet), along with exercise, frequently helps these conditions. Many problems may be unfairly blamed on fatness since so many studies include only those fat people who have been on constant diets: it is not clear in such circumstances whether we are measuring the risk of being fat or the risk of chronic dieting. Many fat people who do not diet but who do exercise regularly are extremely healthy.

In America, a panel convened by the National Institutes of Health proclaimed that obesity was 'a killer disease'. That is a disturbing label: no one, however energetic and attractive she may feel, wants to walk around with a killer disease. The conference, held in the early 1980s, concluded that 'the evidence is now overwhelming that obesity, defined as excessive storage of energy in the form of fat, has adverse effects on health and longevity' and it recommended that 34 million Americans needed to lose weight for the sake of their health.

How on earth did they arrive at that figure? What criteria did they use to determine whether or not an individual was overweight? For many years the basis of such assessments has been tables used by the insurance industry to predict mortality rates and thus to set different levels of insurance premiums according to the perceived risks. The most widely used are those of the Metropolitan Life Insurance Company in America (already mentioned) who analysed recorded information about the weights and survival rates of its policy holders and in 1942 produced the first tables of 'ideal' weight ranges which were supposed to be conducive to optimum life expectancy. By 1959 the tables were described as 'desirable' rather than 'ideal' weight ranges for different heights, which was less dictatorial, but by the 1980s they were simply accepted as the 'Height and Weight Tables', with no qualifying adjective to temper their authority. The assumption is generally made that your life expectancy is reduced if your weight is greater than the range given for your height. But the theories on which the tables are based are not necessarily sound and are far too generalized. For example, they take no account of genetic background, or the age at which weight is gained. In recent years the Gerontology Research Center in Baltimore, Maryland, has looked rather more closely at the raw data used in compiling the insurance tables and has found that age *does* make a difference: weight gained in early adulthood seems to be more conducive to ill health than weight gained later on, and the people with the best life expectancy tend to gain something like an average of a pound a year from 25 to 65 years old.

In 1960 Dr Ancel Keys, of the University of Minnesota, set up an ambitious co-ordinated fifteen-year study in seven countries looking at the effect of weight on mortality, and he was finally able to conclude that, for middle-aged men, the likelihood of dying early was greatest for those who started out lean, and was lowest for the moderately fat. Dr Keys stated: 'Men somewhat heavier than average have the best prospect of avoiding premature death. The popular insurance company claim about mortality is grossly wrong.'

In 1980 a study of middle-aged Swedish women by

H. Noppa *et al.* found that their death rate fell with increasing fatness, even at the upper extremes of obesity. The underweight seem to be much more likely to die than the overweight of the same age; and that, as Paul Ernsberger of Cornell Medical College pointed out in a 1986 article in *Radiance*, is something your great-grandmother could have told you. She would have rated the longevity potential much higher for a large, robust, well nourished woman, five foot seven tall and weighing 224 pounds, than a *Playboy* model of the same height but only half the weight.

The Gerontology Research Center also implied that weight ranges should be the same regardless of sex, i.e. that women, with their generally lighter bones and muscles, could be relatively fatter than men without detriment to their life expectancy. In addition, the tables drawn up in Baltimore gave much wider ranges for each age group. Other studies have considered whether the site of fat deposits on the body makes a difference, and it does seem that the typical accumulation of a 'spare tyre' in middle age is more likely to be associated with health problems than if the same amount of fat is more evenly distributed.

The health risks of overweight depend on how obesity is defined. The severely obese, as I have said, do indeed face a greater risk of high blood-pressure and adult diabetes, but there is controversy about whether or not too much body fat also increases the risk of heart attacks. An article in the Harvard Medical School *Health Letter* in 1986 ('The problem of overweight') queried some of the assumptions made which connected overweight with various conditions of ill health and early mortality, and pointed out, *inter alia*, that 'the American people have been getting somewhat fatter, on the whole, during the past few decades, yet their life expectancy has continued to increase.' The article, with a commendable example of lateral thinking, suggested that a potential health hazard for many overweight people results from the 'discrimination, prejudice and exploitation that they often experience' – including the typical reaction of a doctor to an overweight patient who is assumed to be unco-operative if she fails to lose weight. Indeed, it is sometimes the case that the doctor, having labelled the patient as awkward, tends to be less sympathetic and therefore perhaps less conscientious with her health care.

In spite of all that, the mental health of the overweight seems to stand up very well, apart from a lack of self-esteem because of constant discrimination by parents, friends, employers and society in general. But this lack of confidence makes the overweight person, especially a woman, vulnerable to the persuasiveness of the massive commercial slimming industry: far more harm is probably done by the influence of that industry than by the effects of obesity itself on physical health in the first place. As Ernsberger points out, many of the health problems commonly associated with fatness are probably caused by fat people's incessant pursuit of thinness. He describes this as the 'yoyo syndrome', that deadly cycle of weight loss and weight gain which may cause hypertension. Diet pills can cause high blood-pressure and vitamin psychosis; low-carbohydrate diets may raise cholesterol levels; and liquid protein diets have led to heart disease and sudden death. He says: 'We don't know how unhealthy overweight is of itself, because most overweight people have been doing these things.' Indeed, the old studies overlooked the fact that large people are much more likely to be dieting than thin people. Instead of looking at the differences between fat and thin, they were looking at the differences between dieters and non-dieters.

When so much information from so-called experts is saying that fatness is correlated with ill health, it is extremely satisfying and rewarding to be able to put forward evidence to the contrary. As Susan Wooley says, 'A person can definitely be fat and healthy. There is a very sizeable weight range in which extra weight does not constitute a risk in mortality.' She notes that some studies have shown that women can weigh up to 200 pounds without increasing their mortality risk, and even after that point, she says, being overweight may be healthier than dieting. She goes on: 'In general the healthiest eaters we see are fat women. Most would have to be on a starvation diet for their whole lives to get them down to a weight the culture considers normal and the physical and emotional effects of starvation are much worse than the effects of overweight.'

The risks associated with thinness are given far less media attention. In fact, unusually thin people tend to die young, largely because of an increased cancer risk. Thinner people are also susceptible to lung diseases such as emphysema, fatal infections such as tuberculosis and other problems such as ulcers, anaemia and osteoporosis. Thin women are much more likely to give birth to premature and under-developed babies, too. During the sixties women who were pregnant were put on diets of 2000 calories a day by doctors in order to ensure they did not put on too much weight through the pregnancy, but this practice ceased when it was found to produce undernourished babies. It was yet another example of the medical profession following a fad and carrying out experiments on people which proved to be dangerous.

Little research has been done on the connection between underweight and illness, but Ernsberger believes that poor health is not caused by natural thinness, as in a person with thin parents and grandparents; instead, he suggests that thin people who are unhealthy are probably starving themselves to stay slim. This hypothesis, however, remains to be tested.

The figures for suicide rates are intriguing. They are noticeably lower in the obese, for both men and women. If obese and non-obese people committed suicide at similar rates, each would be represented by a base-rate of 100 per cent. Instead, the figures are 73 per cent for obese women and 78 per cent for obese men, according to Jean Mayer in *Obesity*. The figures have never yet been explained, but it would seem that, in a way not yet understood, the obese have the advantage in mental health.

Thin people are not oppressed for their size in the way that large people are, yet it would seem that it is unhealthy for a large woman whose parents and grandparents were also large to try and be thin. And there are benefits to be gained from extra body fat. For example, large women tend to survive trauma better: they have more body reserves.

Women tend naturally to be fatter than men and can find advantages in being so. The menopause can be a gentler transition for those whose oestrogen levels reduce only gradually at this time of life, so that they become less fertile by degrees rather than by a sudden drop. Oestrogen production takes place in the fat tissues and it is stored there: fat and fertility go hand in hand. Young women start to accumulate body fat in tune with their genetically set clock and some scientists believe there is a minimum amount of fat necessary for the onset of menstruation in the first place. Dr Rose E. Frisch of Harvard University, for example, suggests that the amount of fat on an average eighteen-year-old is just enough to see her through nine months of pregnancy and three months of breast-feeding. Humans have always been faced with possible periods of famine and it is biologically sensible to store enough fat to ensure successful reproduction in spite of food shortages.

Dr Frisch points out in her article 'Fatness and Fertility', published in *Scientific American* in March 1988, that excessively thin women (not necessarily anorexic) often suffer from menstrual disorders which are a direct result of lack of fat. Poor nutrition (for example, severe dieting) and intensive physical exercise affect the activity of the hypothalamus which, as we have already seen, regulates various basic bodily functions, including reproduction. A thin girl will be inclined to mature at a later age, delaying the menarche (the first menstrual cycle), and a very thin woman may suffer from an absence of menstrual cycles and from infertility. As Frisch remarks, historically all the symbols of female fertility have been fat, especially in the breasts, hips, thighs and buttocks – parts of the body where the female sex hormone, oestrogen, promotes the storage of fat. Primitive women would have had a selective advantage if they conceived only when their body reserves were adequate to sustain the pregnancy and subsequent lactation (it takes something between 50,000 and

80,000 extra calories to produce a viable baby and an additional 500 to 1000 calories every day for lactation). Breast milk used to be a newborn child's only source of nutrition, and if a mother lacked a good store of fat she would be quite unable to feed her baby or even develop the foetus when food was scarce. It may well be that today's women, whose mature bodies are composed of more than a quarter of their total weight in fat, have inherited that capacity to store fat precisely in order to provide energy for pregnancy and lactation. By contrast, mature men have only 12 to 14 per cent of their weight stored as fat.

Incidentally, it seems to be a natural human emotion to equate plumpness with comforting maternalism. Cuddly grannies are well-padded rather than skinny; motherly nurses who bring reassurance to vulnerable hospital patients tend to be rounded rather than angular. I wonder, idly, whether any researchers have investigated the psychological effects on a child of having a very thin mother? Ample laps and generous breasts are perhaps what children seek.

A century ago, the average age of menarche was 15.5 years, but now the average for American girls has dropped to 12.6 years. Frisch and her colleague, Roger Revelle of Harvard University, postulate that the earlier menarche 'is explained by the fact that children now become bigger sooner, because they are better nourished and have less disease'. Looking at the diet, growth and reproduction of women in Britain during the mid-1800s, she found that undernourished women matured more slowly, had a later menarche, reached a later peak of fertility, had a lower number of live births in each age group and were much more likely to have unsuccessful pregnancies. There was also a longer interval between births because they suffered a longer period of amenorrhea during breastfeeding, and their age of menopause was early, too. It is noticeable that poor couples in developing countries today also have a lower successful birth rate, largely because the women are undernourished and perform hard physical labour on inadequate diets. Taking all these areas of research together, it seems that weight is the factor that determines the age of menarche and also has a strong influence on a woman's subsequent menstrual pattern.

Osteoporosis, or thin bones, is a problem for many post-menopausal women and this, too, can be affected by body weight. Bone is very much a living substance and its strength is determined by a balanced system of oestrogen, vitamin D and calcium. With the system in balance, oestrogen acts as a catalyst enabling the replacement of calcium laid down on the bone. With osteoporosis, the natural sudden drop in oestrogen levels at menopause tends to leave the bones brittle so that they fracture easily, and in some cases there is pain and a degree of disablement as well. Osteoporosis is part of the natural ageing process, but the bones can be strengthened by regular exercise, a balanced diet with calcium and magnesium in appropriate proportions, and adequate intake of vitamin D – the sunshine vitamin. Extra body mass puts weight on the bones and encourages them to remain stronger. Thin women, whose hormonal system has anyway been out of balance during their lives, are more likely to have an early menopause and hence an earlier risk of osteoporosis, and women who have intentionally kept their weight at a minumum (for example, models and dancers) are beginning to experience problems with osteoporosis at a much earlier age than those who have kept their weight at a more sensible level.

Being thin may not be so healthy after all!

5

GOOD INSIDE

As a practising psychotherapist, I have been working since 1984 with women who have a variety of eating problems. It seems to me that, throughout society as a whole, many women are almost obsessed with food, with how much they take in and what they take in. The people who came to see me were usually large, unhappy with their size, and eating inappropriately; they would very often feel hungry all the time, or they would have lost the ability to heed their body messages and would therefore be eating constantly, usually in response to a need which was nothing to do with hunger and food. For example, if something happened in response to which they felt unhappy or angry, then instead of expressing those emotions they would eat; the feelings suppressed in this way would be less of an immediate problem.

The majority of these women felt very unhappy about their physical size, and their own feelings of poor body image were heightened by the prejudices of society. Many of them would virtually ignore their bodies from the neck downwards, as if they did not exist; they would even arrange mirrors so that they could not see themselves below the neck. Individual eating patterns would vary, but were similar in that they were not eating in response to hunger, they were eating food indiscriminately, and very often they would eat things which society declared were 'naughty but nice': they would have a tremendous urge to eat sweet things like chocolate or cakes or biscuits. Such would be their craving for certain foods that if they bought a box of chocolates or a packet of biscuits, they would eat the lot in one go. There was no sense of enjoyment in their eating: it was much more a feeling of uncontrollable need, and a typical description they gave would be 'eating for the sake of it'. They did not really want the food but could not refrain from eating it.

Generally speaking (and it should be stressed that I am generalizing), a lot of the women who came to see me had such poor self-esteem that they were not taking care of themselves in the way of buying clothes that suited them, having their hair done in styles which they liked, wearing make-up that they enjoyed, buying themselves attractive underwear, or doing things that pleased *them*. They were not involved in sporting activities because they were too embarrassed to wear the clothes or could not find anything suitable. Susie Orbach, who has done so much work on women with eating problems, describes similar attitudes in *Fat is a Feminist Issue*.

These are the type of women relevant to this book, though I also work with women who have problems with anorexia.

During my work to help these women improve their

self-image, I generally came to realize that when they had discarded their inappropriate eating patterns and were eating a well-balanced, nutritious diet, they found that their weight and size did not necessarily decrease to any significant degree, although very often they were eating less than the slim people they lived and worked with. They might lose some weight but would settle at what society would still deem a large size.

This mirrored my own experience when I stopped eating inappropriately and began to deal with my feelings rather than eating my way around them. I had worked through this stage myself and could identify with the realization that, although I had come to terms with my own body and emotions and was at last eating appropriately, other people assumed I still had a problem and implied that, because of my size, I must still be eating a great deal more than anybody else.

I knew that this was not true of myself and I decided to test my own experience by asking the women who came to me for therapy to join me in keeping diaries of our food intake. I realized that there would be discrepancies in the diaries; certainly to begin with it is easy to be dishonest with yourself, but I knew that my own discrepancies had decreased as I felt better about myself, and as my self-esteem grew the records I kept became more honest and accurate. I checked other women's diaries periodically and noticed a similar improvement in their record-keeping.

It became obvious that the women were eating appropriately over long periods and so we could prove that we were not greedy or self-indulgent or out of control of our eating. We could show that we no longer had problems with food. The problem now was the assumptions made by other people. We had successfully struggled to change our eating habits but were still feeling very fragile with our new sense of self-esteem and belief in ourselves, only to be faced with erroneous assumptions by other people, very often voiced quite plainly . 'Oh, Margaret will have a second helping' is typical of the less offensive comments.

This was the stage at which I felt women needed moral support and that is why I devised the first Big and Beautiful workshops.

Initially they were tried out as single-day workshops, run under the auspices of the University of Southampton's Department of Adult Education and based in Southampton and Winchester. I also ran some at the Spectrum organization in north London. I made it clear that we were not looking at the issue of eating problems and how women could deal with those, but were more concerned with how women could deal with the prejudicial attitudes and oppression they had to face. My ideas developed into the longer-term workshops I now run in London and Hampshire.

The information leaflet that I hand out to those who express interest in the workshops states right at the beginning that research shows that about half of British women are size 16 or over and that the workshop is especially for them, but I emphasize that the workshop is about 'feeling good and looking great rather than dieting or disguising our size'. I say that no matter how you feel about yourself *inside*, in our society very often being large is seen as being unhealthy, lazy, greedy, self-indulgent, lacking in will-power and above all a failure, and that the course sets out to challenge those attitudes. The issues we will explore include waiting to be thin before we feel able to embark on some activity that attracts us (95 per cent of diets do not work); attitudes in the media, fashion industry and society and how they affect us; the historical perspective; how we can help ourselves practically and emotionally. 'We plan to celebrate our size, not apologize for it,' I tell them. 'Why not join us?'

When a women decides to join one of my Big and Beautiful workshops, she has already taken the first positive step towards recovering her self-esteem and, by opening women's eyes to new ideas, we can begin to celebrate size rather than be ashamed of it. Being large is not abnormal and large women do not have to feel isolated, timid and afraid. The workshops prove that a lot of other women feel the same about themselves, and have to varying degrees lost their self-respect, but by sharing their feelings they begin to realize that they are not alone, they are not odd or strange or wrong. They are not the ones who are out of step; they do not have to conform and squeeze themselves into society's moulds. The workshops stress that being acceptable to other people is not the most important thing in the world: it is much more important to be able to accept yourself.

Women who try to become thin by dieting are not failing at something which is easy, nor is what they are attempting appropriate. Although in our culture such a high percentage of the population put themselves on diets of one kind or another, reducing their food intake to deal with some particular aspect of their body which displeases them, it is never easy. Bearing in mind the reasons why dieting does not work, outlined in previous chapters, and the way in which women often either return to their original weight after dieting or even become heavier, it is clear that dieters are almost bound to fail.

Nancy Worcester, in her book *Women and Food*, puts the matter into perspective when she explains that in attempting to change food habits we are tackling one of our most conservative behaviour patterns, and one which is strongly linked to our inner sense of security. It is noticeable, for example, that immigrants adapting to a new lifestyle persist in their homeland eating habits long after they have changed in other ways to fit in with the new environment. Rituals concerned with eating are very much related to the sense of self and if we look at different cultures, or even different families, we can recognize the rituals which grow up around food and eating within that group. It is therefore a particularly difficult challenge to try and change the pattern of your food consumption. Unlike smoking or drinking, it is impossible to abstain completely: we do not have the option to give up food, only to change our eating habits.

It is especially difficult for women. Even today it is still traditionally the woman who deals with the family's food in many households: she chooses the menu, shops, cooks, prepares and serves the food, and clears up after the meal. In such a role it is very hard indeed for her to ignore her own hunger pangs and preoccupation with her diet. But when a woman comes to one of the workshops in despair at the endless carousel of dieting, she has at least begun to address her problem.

A day-long workshop starts with an introduction about my own background and how and why I am actually running the course. Then we introduce ourselves to one another by sharing names. We are in a warm, pleasant, comfortable environment because it is important that everyone should be able to feel relaxed, and we group ourselves in a circle to increase the informality. I explain that the intention is not for me to lecture them but for all of us to have the opportunity of sharing our experiences and giving each other support. This sharing of ideas and support is the essence of the workshops and we put a 'circle of confidentiality' around the group so that everyone understands she can talk outside the group about what she did or said or felt during the sessions but she does not discuss what anybody else feels. This is not because we expect anyone to reveal highly personal details, but because it is important that the women feel safe to say what they like and to know that it will not be repeated outside. Some women question that, but all respect the safety that it gives them to express themselves as and how they want.

Then we break up into small groups to discuss the general question: 'Do society's attitudes affect us and, if so, how?' This raises plenty of discussion; women talk about how they have been personally affected and recount situations they have faced – for example how their mothers had insisted on them wearing dark, shapeless clothes, how they now find it difficult to select clothes especially when faced by a slim young assistant who makes disdainful comments. They nearly always talk about the concept of waiting to be thin, the fact that 95 per cent of diets do not work, the common experience of seesawing between stringent punitive dieting and then putting the weight on again and how unhealthy this can be, and the general question of just how unhealthy being large really is anyway. We consider the stress of facing a constant barrage of prejudice and how such stress can play havoc with our health.

We talk about fashionable body shapes and how they vary in different parts of the world and have changed in the course of history; we note, for example, that in the late 19th century three acceptable types (the frail, the voluptuous and the athletic) seemed to co-exist but somehow society has now restricted itself to only one idea. Invariably the women cite famous movie stars from the past like Jane Russell, Marilyn Monroe and other voluptuous women who were considered desirable and beautiful in their day but might now be considered fat.

The other figure who always enters the conversation at this point is Twiggy, who precipitated a tidal wave of fashionable thinness in the 1960s. Then the discussion often turns to the media – how advertisements nearly always feature very slim women; how being lean is always equated with being successful, affluent and good at your job, with the implication that large is the reverse; how magazines often feature articles on anorexia alongside advertisements for slimming aids and diets that promise a different way of life; how these products are often endorsed by media stars to increase the fantasy, and how the whole business amounts to a massive onslaught of propaganda aimed at women.

Discrimination at work is another subject which is always aired, especially how women believe that their career prospects are impaired by their size. Then there is the universal problem of lack of consideration in public places, such as the difficulty of fitting into fixed seats or wearing seatbelts.

This far-ranging discussion takes up a fair proportion of the morning, then we have a break. I provide coffee, tea, soft drinks and biscuits (including chocolate ones), and one woman commented, 'This is probably the only place that I can eat a chocolate biscuit without feeling embarrassed or that I should feel ashamed!'

After the break we go into more detail about the historical perspective and the various ways in which women in the past have used padding or corseting to try and conform with the ideal shape of their time, and occasionally a woman will share her experience of such present-day surgical methods as jaw-wiring. (I have never met a woman who has retained her lower weight after the wires have been removed: all of them talk about regaining weight slowly but unfailingly as soon as they return to an ordinary nutritious diet.)

That leads on to talking about health, and whether or not being large is unhealthy. Sometimes there is disagreement about this: some women are very concerned about their weight from a health point of view and others challenge the idea that being large automatically means being unhealthy. The discussion turns naturally to ways of maintaining health and well-being, and attention often focuses on exercise. There are conversations about the most appropriate exercise for large people and, although only one or two take part in sport regularly, most women say they have at least tried walking. However, the majority express tremendous reluctance to become involved in any activity at a sports centre because they have not practised any sport for a long time, maybe not since their schooldays and certainly not since they became large. Many claim this is because they cannot find nice-looking sportswear and also because they fear ridicule. For instance, swimming is recommended as a good sport for large people but for a large woman whose self-esteem is still a little fragile the act of putting on a swimsuit, walking out into a public swimming area and getting into the water can be a considerable challenge. Even thinking about it can be frightening for some of them.

Many of the women say that if they could find more attractive things to wear, then they would be more encouraged to participate in sport. There are always some people, like myself, who say, 'To hang with society and its attitudes, I'll do what sport I want to do.' I usually talk about windsurfing and canoeing, two sports I enjoy, and how I swim as often as I can because I adore it.

At this point we begin to share ways of feeling good about ourselves – what I call pampering and looking after yourself – and these include various ways of being kind to ourselves and helping ourselves to feel good. Very often this leads to the question of being selfish. Basically, people who already have low self-esteem have great difficulty in devoting time and energy to themselves, but some of us are prepared to challenge that, saying that if we do not take care of ourselves and feel good about ourselves we are not going to be able to help other people or be pleasant companions anyway. Put like that, 'selfishness' sounds very unselfish!

Women talk about yoga as being a good way of keeping supple – if only they can pluck up the courage to join a class. We talk about specific exercises in suppleness and the improvement of muscle tone, rather than those designed to reduce weight or size.

It is at this point that we usually discuss doctors' attitudes, which can be summed up by two common experiences: that the medical profession tells us everything can be blamed on our size and weight, whatever the real complaint might be, and that doctors do not treat who we are but who they think we should be, giving us the feeling that we are neither heeded nor respected. Women get quite angry about this; the discussion is often very heated, and I think it is good that they are able to express and share their anger. They are encouraged by realizing they are not alone in being treated like this, and that will help them to feel more able to challenge these attitudes when they next meet them.

The afternoon begins with more practical matters. In the first session we look at my clothes and note that discussions among large women very quickly come round to the problem of how to look good. This is not in order to try and please anyone else but to boost our own morale: everyone, male or female and regardless of their size, recognizes that they feel better if they think they look better – perhaps by having a haircut, or buying themselves something nice to wear. It is not about dressing for somebody else's benefit; it is about dressing to *feel* good. And all large women will bemoan the fact that they cannot get what they want to wear in their size. I appreciate that the situation is improving, but it is still not good enough and my experience in these workshops bears this out. The women always talk about the problem of getting clothes and complain that what they are offered is dowdy and frumpy. So we discuss how we can break the stereotype, how we can start dressing to suit ourselves and to reflect the way we feel. It is a question of finding our own style.

I ask for a volunteer and use a set of neckline shapes which we can all try on in front of a mirror to see how different necklines can look good on one person but not on another. We find that style is not about size but about shape and proportion. We also spend time as a group trying on each other's clothes so that women can experiment. They may see another woman in an outfit which they really like but have never dared to try on. The women spontaneously start swapping clothes and trying on different things; they admire each other's clothes and share ideas and information, being very supportive, saying to each other, 'I think this would really suit you,' or 'I really like that.' They begin to notice that an outfit that suits one size 26 woman will not suit another, and that the effect is not determined by size or even by colour but by proportion.

After a mid-afternoon break, we disperse into small groups again to consider the question: 'Well, what now? What are we going to *do* about it? What physical action are we going to take to challenge society's attitudes?' We start by examining the situation at home and coming up with ideas about talking to our loved ones about how unkind and hurtful some of their discriminatory remarks can be, however well-meaning and caring their intentions or however much they believe they are in our best interests. We talk about how women can support their children if they are large and come up against similar problems.

Turning from the home front, we tackle the question of complaining in shops – not just grumbling to an assistant but asking to see someone in authority so that we can make constructive complaints, pointing out for example that if they had clothes in our size then we would buy them and they would have a new customer.

We talk about writing to the producers of television programmes and commercials, and to the editors of magazines and newspapers, to express disquiet about dieting features, particularly when they are combined with stories about anorexia, for instance. Again the golden rule is to always go to the top. If you are going to make the effort to write, it is well worth making the effort to write to someone who can actually deal with the problem and change something.

The result of the session is practical ideas for challenging society's attitudes and prejudices. There is a lot more anger during this session; it has probably been building up for years, but the women say that they have always become upset rather than been able to express their anger positively. It is good to recognize and express suppressed anger, and these practical sessions at the workshop give them one kind of opportunity to do so. After that we wind up the day with a brief relaxation exercise.

This is just an outline of a typical day-long workshop. I run other courses on a weekly basis over four or six weeks and these are about the positive acceptance of your own body. We use visualization techniques based on Marcia Germaine Hutchinson's book *Transforming Body Image: Learning to Love the Body You Have*. We begin with simple exercises to encourage women to develop and use their skills of imagination so that they can get in touch with how they feel about their bodies and then recognize that they can learn to feel better about them. They are encouraged to concentrate on how they *feel* about themselves at the present time, and not about how they *look*. After that they can start identifying how they *want* to feel, gathering together a set of emotional choices that they wish to make true for themselves.

These exercises explore how we feel about different parts of our bodies, identifying areas that we do not feel good about and changing those feelings so that we can choose to feel good about ourselves in general. It is not about changing our outward appearance at all, but changing our feelings towards ourselves. We explore how we came to have a negative body image; we trace our lives back through childhood and begin to recognize what it was like to be us in that life, to imagine and feel what it was like to be us in that life at a given time. We recall the messages we received about how to be a woman in the world and what a woman was supposed to look like and feel like.

Some of the exercises are designed to enable women to recognize how their own negative self-images confine and restrict them, how they subconsciously make decisions based on those negative feelings and assume that other people will feel the same way. We use affirmations which women create for themselves; we encourage them to have good, healthy relationships with their bodies, to be able to care for them and nurture them, and to feel good about doing so.

I am not suggesting that women leave my workshops in any way 'cured'. This is a learning experience; the workshops are to help women to help themselves. It is an ongoing process in which each woman needs to find her own ways of exploring what is happening for her and recognizing why she feels uncomfortable with her body, and to use the various skills and experiences provided by the exercises for her own benefit in her own way.

When a woman comes to a workshop in despair at the endless dieting carousel, she has at least begun to address her problem, and by sharing it she gains encouragement to persist, though perhaps not in quite the way she expected. Very often the first step she is asked to take is to agree *not* to concentrate on her size. Thinking about dieting, thinking about size, automatically introduces the idea of food and distracts her from concentrating on other areas of her life. The most liberating gift many women can give themselves is the decision that they are no longer going to try and lose weight. Until that decision is made, it is tempting to put off everything else and in the meantime both to dislike oneself and to see the fat as a failure which is carried around with you wherever you go. In other words, walking around the size you are constantly reminds you (if your aim is to be smaller) that you are a failure. When a woman feels a failure in one area of her life, it is very easy to transfer that feeling on to the rest of her life as well. While she continues to despise her body, she is wasting her potential energy.

We ask a woman to look at herself instead as a whole human being and we suggest, for a start, that she should stop weighing herself and get rid of the idea that her weight is the most important thing in her life. It is not. She is a whole person, living, breathing, having relationships, playing her part in the world. What is the rest of her life like? Can she focus on other areas of it which she can feel good about, or other areas which she would like to change? Is her concern with her weight an excuse for not facing up to other realities? Are there other options she could explore or other choices she might make?

None of this is imposed: I believe that every woman

Examples from the Edwardian era of what was then the ideal and desirable image of womanhood

Left: Chalcolithic goddess of fertility - a female figure of worship from a past age

Below: A familiar situation to every woman of size 16 or over – but with a new response

Assistant: 'I'M AFRAID WE HAVEN'T ANYTHING IN YOUR SIZE, MADAM.'
Piqued Lady: 'WELL, WE AIN'T *ALL* RUN UP OUT OF REMNANTS, YOU KNOW.'

A typical example of postcard humour which ridicules large women

The stereotypical image of a large, overbearing wife and hen-pecked husband is reinforced

The different visual effects achieved by varying neckline and accessories, clearly shown in these two photographs of the author

has a right to choose whether she wants to change or not. But it is often the case that a woman is so fixated on the belief that she is fat and unacceptable that she fails to recognize what else is going on in her life.

Diet is important, of course, but there is a clear difference between a weight-reducing diet and a change of diet to improve nutrition. It is much more important to eat more whole grains and vegetables, more foods rich in iron and calcium, and to cut down on sugary, salt-laden or highly processed foods – not because they affect size but because they affect health. The emphasis should be on nutritional benefit, health and well-being, with little or no reference to reducing weight.

Many women feel so bad about their own bodies that they ignore or deride them. They look after their faces and their hair but wear clothes without any thought about whether they are suitable or whether they feel good in an outfit. They lose touch with their bodies; they do not listen to them. If they are dieting and feeling hungry all the time, they are failing to respond to their bodies; if they did so, they would eat. When they become more attuned to their bodies again, they will eat when it is appropriate and when their bodies tell them to.

Of course it is difficult. Few women choose to risk conflict with the dominant culture which tells them they should be thin, and there is a crying need for this constricting equation of beauty with thinness to be challenged. First we need to close our mouths – not to food but to the incessant discussion of diets and weight. We should stop using numbers of pounds lost as an index of achievement, and should stop complimenting each other on weight loss. Then we should open our mouths: we should talk about our behaviour, be it dieting, bingeing and purging, or continually thinking about food; we should talk about disliking or even being disgusted by certain parts of our body; we should talk about our furtive daily climb onto the scales for compulsive weighing. Once a social problem becomes a public issue, it ceases to be a private agony; and this is as true of size concern as it is of incest, rape or wife-battering.

We certainly need to challenge the idea that we will be happy when we are thin. We must look critically at the emaciated models in the media and, rather than being envious, we should recognize them as exploitative and reject them. Thinness is merely a passing fashion, and if too many women become thin no doubt the pendulum will swing back so that big will be beautiful again. Beauty really does lie in the eye of the beholder, and we can create our own standards of beauty which embrace all shapes and sizes. As long as we continue to try to conform, we are neglecting the nourishment of our growth as *people*.

'You look fat and fresh today,' is a complimentary greeting from a Punjabi Indian. It is time we began giving compliments to our friends, and to ourselves, which are positive about size or which do not refer to size at all.

Once a woman can accept her size, she can begin to feel more comfortable about herself. Very often, as she begins to feel good inside, her weight settles down instead of seesawing violently according to the diet regime of the moment. Many people still expect a woman to reduce automatically to an 'ideal' size at this point. This might happen but not necessarily, and we need to accept that we might remain larger than the world expects, and that to do so is fine as long as we feel 'good in our skin', as the Greek phrase puts it. Quiet self-confidence can be a very attractive characteristic.

Part of that acceptance is gained by loving and nourishing our bodies rather than despising them. In the workshops we talk about ways of self-nourishment, such as buying nice clothes and underwear, or wearing a delicious perfume, or having our hair done. Sometimes we talk about the cost of such things and then consider things which cost little or nothing except effort, like having a pleasant shower, relaxing with a good book, taking a long, luxurious bath, or becoming involved in an enjoyable activity – it does not matter what it is, as long as it is not eating! Some women talk about soft lights, candles, scented baths, a relaxing drink. The idea is to take time out to pamper ourselves, to do what we want to do, to be involved in an activity which is totally and purely for *us*.

Another subject we discuss in the workshops is therapeutic massage (nothing to do with massage parlours). At first women are usually reticent and shy: many large women are wary of physical contact because of their negative feelings about their bodies. However, all human beings need tactile contact with other people and massage is one way of achieving it. Some of the women have practised this on each other very successfully and with great mutual benefit. Massage is a technique for relaxing and toning tense muscles and can leave the body feeling both relaxed and invigorated; at the same time it proves to a large woman that her body is acceptable and she need not despise it.

Taking time out of a busy routine to take more care of themselves and do things they want to do – not to steal time but to give it to themselves generously – helps large women to shed the victim syndrome. Finding this time often requires negotiation and we therefore need to become more assertive, and ask clearly for what we want. It has to be emphasized that assertion is not the same as aggression: it is the ability to state clearly what you want and then go ahead and achieve it, but at the same time take into account the feelings and needs of other people.

It bears repeating time and time again that we cannot make any changes without loving and caring for ourselves. If we feel bad about our bodies, we neglect them. Such neglect underpins our own negative feelings about ourselves but if we begin to break this down and take care of our bodies, then the body responds and we feel better – not thinner or larger, but fitter, more supple, more accepted, more loved, and good enough to be loved. The emphasis has shifted: rather than trying to reduce our size, we take very positive steps to feel good about our own bodies, whatever their size.

The celebration of size and self generates the notion that though other people's opinions obviously affect us they do not really matter. We can deal with them without our self-confidence being destroyed. In the workshops we build up self-confidence, self-worth and a feeling of congruence – a key word. It means that we no longer pretend to the world that all is well though we actually feel bad inside. Instead, we feel good inside, so that there is no need to pretend. Our outward behaviour reflects our new sense of inner security. We are feeling good, and so we are looking good.

But the whole process of learning to love our bodies takes time and it often helps at first just to pretend to ourselves that we feel good about ourselves, and to treat our bodies accordingly, until imperceptibly we find that we actually do love our bodies. We use body-awareness exercises in the workshops; we practise relaxation techniques which help us be in touch with the whole person and we also place great emphasis on using the imagination. We are often taught that our imagination is concerned with flights of fancy and is nothing like reality, but I disagree. I have experienced imaginary happenings which have caused my body to reframe itself physiologically in response to what I imagine. During my pregnancy, for example, I remember being taken through a guided fantasy of lying comfortably relaxed in a field on a warm summer's day, hearing the breeze whispering softly through the grass and feeling the warm sunshine on my face – and I could hear the grass and feel the sun, as I would if I were actually lying in the field. My body had the physical sensations of those feelings; I felt so relaxed and happy that I was quite reluctant to return to the reality of the antenatal clinic.

One can use unpleasant imagery too. Imagine you are standing on a window ledge, several storeys above a street so far away that the people and cars are like ants. You dare not move; you are so precariously balanced that a false move might send you plummeting to the pavement below. If you monitor the sensations and changes that take place in your body and your mental state, you will be aware of the fear, or even terror: a heightened heart-beat, clammy hands, sweating body – yes, the actual physical symptoms of fear will be there. That is how powerful our imaginations can be.

That power can be used in various ways in the workshops, and I employ three techniques: spontaneous imagery, guided imagery and controlled imagery, all of them in response to words from me. For example, if I ask you to imagine yourself walking through a field, that is guided imagery: you are constructing very specific images. If I ask you to walk through a passage into a cave where you have never been before and have no idea what to expect, this has elements of spontaneous imagery: you simply let your imagination conjure up spontaneous images, rather like a daydream. If I then ask you to change the environment or to change the objects in the cave around in a specific way, that is controlled imagery.

Some people find it difficult to use their imagination, and some people find certain types of imagery more difficult than others. All the senses come into imagery and, again, some people find some senses easier to imagine than others: some people can see images more clearly than they can smell them, or some can feel imaginary textures like satin and velvet more readily than they can hear imaginary sounds.

All can improve with practice if they are willing to keep trying. Some people are at first rather dismissive or sceptical about the use of imagery in this work but are usually prepared at least to give it a try, and all the women I have worked with have found it useful in varying degrees. We can use imagery to explore our bodies physically and emotionally, and to readjust and reform our feelings and attitudes towards ourselves.

It is a technique which is difficult to describe in

words: it needs to be experienced, rather like undertaking a journey on a new route we know we shall be using regularly. At first we have a map or write down a set of instructions, and we refer frequently to this paper guidance when we first use the route. The more often we do the journey, the less we refer to the map. But then suppose we do the same journey as a navigator rather than driving ourselves. It is quite difficult, even if as drivers we are fairly familiar with the route. There are sensations and memories in the body which can be recalled when driving but which are more difficult to recall when navigating someone else. This is the 'felt image', or information which is gained through physical experience and not by the written word, so that when we drive under our own navigation we have an extra ability to remember. Think how difficult it is to explain to a beginner how to change gear: it is something you do automatically hundreds of times on a journey, but without thinking, and, like the art of riding a bicycle, it is quite hard to convey the physical motions and sensations to someone who has not experienced them.

And that is why I use imagery in the workshops: it gives women their own 'felt image', which will be much more effective for them than just talking.

After the imagery work, the next step is self-affirmation: I encourage women to write down positive choices about how they want to feel about themselves – a statement of self-affirmation and intent. Like so many of the techniques we use in the workshops, this is most beneficial in a group situation: it is much more difficult to do it alone, though after an initial experience in a group (or at least with a partner) they can then go and practise by themselves if they wish.

We also deal with anger. It is easy for large people to come to the conclusion that they might as well not take care of themselves in terms of nutrition and exercise because the medical world has already decided they are going to die young. We use the workshops to destroy the myths and challenge the assumption of a correlation between fat and bad health, and we enable women to become angry with the perpetrators of the myths. It can be very releasing for a woman to get in touch with her anger rather than the usual feelings of guilt and oppression; it is difficult for her to feel good about herself and take care of herself if she is burdened by unexpressed feelings like anger. When women begin to recognize that they can express the feelings, then they have taken the first step towards being able to replace the feelings with self-love and self-confidence.

When I talk about releasing suppressed anger, I am not suggesting that women become aggressive. I am talking about recognizing the reality of what is being done to them and how they are allowing themselves to respond to that. Once they understand that they are not greedy, lazy, selfish and all the other negative descriptions that people use about them, then they can begin to challenge those descriptions assertively rather than aggressively. Aggression is rarely listened to and an aggressive woman is immediately labelled as hysterical, but an assertive woman will be heard.

Part of the pathway to realizing just how much we have been oppressed is to talk about the history of image and how women have in various ways conformed to an acceptable image instead of being true to themselves, and how easy it is to fall into that trap now because we happen to be in a group of people who do not conform to the ideal image.

We look at positive role models, especially well-known large women who have either ignored their size or used it appropriately. For example, there are superb singers like Ella Fitzgerald, Jessye Norman, Bertice Reading and Grace Bumbry. There are powerful athletes like Fatima Whitbread and Tessa Sanderson. There are media personalities like Gloria Hunniford. There is Nancy Roberts, who founded the Spare Tyre Theatre Company in 1979 and who had her own Thames Television series, *Large as Life* and *Nancy at Large*. There is Ann Harper, who became the first 'fuller figure' model in 1978 and is one of the pioneers in her field, presenting an image which is more glamorous than contemporary. Then there are the pictures painted by Beryl Cook, who takes a benevolent and light-hearted look at large women and sees them as attractive, funny and good company rather than judging them for their size.

It can be very difficult for women who are in the public eye. One can certainly think of women who have been quite content with their size until the media searchlight has been turned on them so that, regardless of their initial protestations of self-confidence and contentment with their bodies, they have over a period of time pursued a lifestyle or regime which has reformed their body into a more socially acceptable package. In view of the sniping, vindictive criticism which the media can too readily hand out to women like Elizabeth Taylor, it is of course understandable that some women wilt under the onslaught, but I feel very sad when it happens. Not only is it a betrayal of the woman in question but also, when she is so much in the limelight and is a role model for other women, it is a betrayal of us all.

On a more personal level, I aim to provide a role model myself: I talk about my own ways of nurturing myself, of making space for myself in the day, of self-respect, of making an effort to look good *for myself*.

We also acknowledge what I call the fragile stage, the point at which we are feeling more comfortable in ourselves, only to be faced with the difficulties of other people's attitudes. Once we recognize that this is merely a stage, something we naturally feel vulnerable about but that we can face, then we are ready to go out into the world with a new-found belief in ourselves. Some women expect too much from society: they feel that they have worked so hard to reach this stage that the world should recognize and acclaim their success, and they are deeply disappointed when that does not happen. Others are more realistic and know that they will be challenged, know that people will expect a large woman to feel bad about herself and be irritated because she actually feels good, but they also know they can deal with the challenge.

When a large woman stops wasting all her energies in worrying about dieting and food and about whether or not she is acceptable, then that energy is released for other things and she can become powerful, beneficial to others as well as herself. She is able to challenge the world, and she will be heard.

6

FEELING FIT

When a woman has gained a new confidence and is prepared to celebrate her size and challenge the world, then she is ready to take care of herself and look more positively at fitness, fashion and nutrition.

A large woman has the same basic requirements for a good, balanced diet as anyone else. She needs to forget about her size and to concentrate instead on healthy eating. For a start, she needs to eat regularly rather than to snack. Eat three meals a day, and in particular eat well in the morning rather than skipping breakfast as so many women do. Your body is active during the day and has a chance to use the food beneficially, whereas in the evening you are likely to be sitting around or sleeping, which is not a good way of using what you have eaten.

In recent years people have become much more conscious of the nutritional value of their food and in our workshop discussions we encourage women to forget about counting calories and learn more about the goodness of natural foods. We advocate the least amount of processing: for example, fresh raw vegetables retain more nutrition than those that are frozen and cooked. We discuss ways of cooking food which least diminish the food's value, and explain something about the constituents of different foods and the balance of minerals, vitamins, fat, carbohydrates and protein they contain. It is important that women who have spent so much of their lives seeing food as the enemy should be able to understand the essentials of nutrition and learn to appreciate and enjoy wholesome food. If their bodies are properly cared for and nourished, then their food fantasies will be firmly laid to rest.

The secret of good nutrition is to eat a *balanced* and varied diet based on a general understanding of the body's needs. Very broadly, the essential nutrients in food are proteins, carbohydrates, fats, minerals and vitamins. Water is essential to maintain the body in good health and it is easier to die from lack of water than lack of food.

Proteins are built up from amino acids in various combinations and they are part of the basic material of many body tissues like muscles, skin, hair, nails, various organs, hormones and enzymes. They might also provide energy in some circumstances. The body can manufacture about half of the amino acids it needs to make protein, but the rest, known as 'essential' amino acids, must come from food. Some good sources of protein are chicken, beef, pork, fish, soybean and cottage cheese.

Carbohydrates are substances such as sugar, starch and glycogens. The body can synthesize all its carbohydrates from materials like glucose, fructose and galactose; it can also convert carbohydrates into fat.

The body's usual source of energy comes from the burning of the basic constituents of carbohydrates, i.e. carbon, hydrogen and oxygen, and that energy is essential for muscular work, breathing, body heat and other functions. Some good sources of carbohydrates in the diet are whole grains, fruit, vegetables and honey, but there are many foods which are too high in refined carbohydrates and sugars to be good for the health if consumed on a regular basis or in quantity – including white bread, beer, soft drinks, spirits and of course all the sweet favourites like cakes, biscuits, ice cream, sweets, chocolate, jam, tinned-fruit in syrup and many other desserts and puddings.

Lipids, or fats, provide a source of energy which is twice as concentrated as the same weight of either carbohydrate or protein. They are composed of fatty acids and glycerol and, like amino acids, some of the essential fatty acids needed by the body cannot be manufactured by it and must be obtained from food. These are polyunsaturated fats and are found in foods like vegetable oils, sunflower seeds, certain margarines – and walnuts.

Minerals and vitamins are vital to the body but are only needed in tiny amounts. They must be acquired through the diet but, with a properly balanced diet, it is rarely necessary to take special supplements except in certain circumstances. Indeed, it is possible to suffer ill-effects from overdosage of some vitamins, and I rarely recommend vitamin supplements: it is better to adjust the diet. At one time there was a general craze for taking them and I became very concerned because people were swallowing vitamin pills indiscriminately. Some vitamins are water-soluble and some are fat-soluble. If they are water-soluble then the body can deal with any excess by flushing it through the kidney and bladder system, but fat-soluble vitamins are difficult to get rid of and can build up with unpleasant side-effects. Rather than take supplements, it is much better to eat a varied diet so that a vitamin deficiency in one type of food can be balanced by the vitamin content of another. Fresh vegetables, fruits and grains supply many of the body's needs for vitamins but some occur only in foods of animal origin and are best obtained from lean meat, fish, eggs and dairy-produce. Milk is one of nature's miracle foods: it contains significant amounts of nearly all the nutrients we need.

I give out information sheets about which foods are rich in certain vitamins and also on those that are high in refined carbohydrates and high in sugar (see Appendix I). People seem to find the balance of fat in their diet easy to maintain: they might replace butter with margarine, or cut fat off the meat and remember to grill rather than fry. This is not about reducing weight; it is about having a balanced diet. In general, a balanced diet should include high-fibre foods like wholemeal bread and cereal, beans and pulses, fresh fruit and vegetables, and it makes nutritional sense to eat more poultry and fish and less red meat as well as substituting skimmed or semi-skimmed milk for whole milk.

We should take a lot more care about what goes into our supermarket trolleys, not because of weight-watching but for the sake of good nutrition. And that means thinking about what we are buying and considering what we really need rather than habitually stocking up with what we are used to eating. It means never going shopping when we are hungry because then we tend to buy indiscriminately. Eating is one of our prime bodily functions and nutrition is one of our prime needs, and if we deprive ourselves our bodies react by concentrating our energies and minds on food. For instance, if a hungry policeman walks along his beat he is more likely to notice the food shops, restaurants and cafeterias than he is to be able to pick up any details of other activity in the street. In other words, our bodies fix on their prime needs and if you are hungry and you go shopping then you will probably make inappropriate food-buying choices. We owe it to ourselves (and to our families) to take food seriously and thoughtfully.

It is perhaps ironic that, in agriculture, the rations given to farm livestock of different kinds are very carefully balanced to take account of the individual animal's needs down to the last milligram of minerals, yet a farming family may know far less about its own nutritional requirements. A strong case can be made for including considerably more knowledge about food values in children's basic education.

When we discuss healthy eating in the workshops, some women are concerned that good nutrition will be beyond their means. Traditionally, in poorer families the man eats meat while the woman eats potatoes. As well as encouraging a woman to eat well herself, we try to help each other with the problems of a low budget by exchanging information about local markets for good fresh vegetables or shops where cheap nutritional food can be bought – cheap cuts of meat, perhaps, or vegetarian meals which are often more economical than meat dishes.

To eat properly when money is tight, you need imagination, and some useful cookbooks are shown in the Bibliography. You also need time: shopping and cooking on a low budget take longer, and this can be a major difficulty.

A lot of women are conscious of the effects of 'E numbers' or additives and they take care to check food labels and identify additives so that they can limit the amount ingested as much as possible, especially artificial colouring and preservatives. There are other items which should be limited, too. For example, alcohol, sugar and other refined carbohydrates increase the need for nutrients because they are incomplete foods and the body has to work harder to process them. Salt in excess upsets the delicate balance between potassium and sodium in the body and this can be a cause of higher blood-pressure (something which large women are supposed to be prone to). Excessive caffeine also has harmful effects.

Smoking increases the need for vitamins A, B and C and the minerals zinc and calcium, so that smokers need to look even more carefully at the nutritional value of their diets. Smoking also affects the hormone system and can thus be detrimental to the quality of the skin, particularly in older women.

The aim of our workshop discussions is to encourage women to care for their bodies so that they can be proud of themselves. In most cases self-destructive habits like smoking will soon come to an end once they have accepted their bodies and understood the importance of nourishing them, which is rather more positive than preaching against abuse of the body. So we do not bludgeon people with anti-smoking slogans, but we talk in general terms about the habit being an unhealthy one. We also talk about the widespread belief that if a woman stops smoking her weight will increase. This is not necessarily the case. It is true, however, that when a person gives up smoking it is very easy to substitute it with something else – and that something else is very often food. If a woman decides to give up smoking, therefore, she needs to be cautious and monitor her eating habits to make sure that she does not increase her intake of food inappropriately by snacking all the time. A lot of women substitute cigarettes one for one with sweets and snacks so that when they would normally have a cigarette they will instead have a snack, and very often that snack will be high in fat and/or sugar. We suggest that women have a supply of appropriate snacks around, like pieces of fruit, sesame seed, or raw vegetables. Women come up with numerous ideas about what they can have if they need a substitute for a cigarette.

It is also true that some women find that, in order to give up cigarettes in the first place, they do allow themselves to eat inappropriately for a while. Providing this is a short-term solution which they grant themselves on a temporary basis before reverting to more beneficial eating habits, then that is fine.

A major component in feeling good about your body is feeling fit: exercise is also vital to a sense of well-being. The emphasis should be on feeling well, not on body image. There are several questions you can ask yourself to assess how fit you are. For example, do you feel stiff in the morning after taking exercise the day before? Are you supple enough for day-to-day activities? Do you often feel tired even if you have done nothing physically tiring, or do you often find it difficult to get to sleep although you feel overtired? Do you get breathless when you run for the bus, or when you have climbed two flights of stairs, so that you have to pause for a few minutes before you can talk? Do you sometimes feel depressed for no particular reason? If you answer 'yes' to several of these questions, your fitness is not what it might be and you can take steps to improve it so that your body can do whatever you reasonably require of it without becoming exhausted.

During our workshops we encourage women to choose an activity they have always wanted to do but have avoided because of their size, and then we encourage them to go ahead and *do* it. This can be a very exciting step but it can also be frightening. Women often decide to form their own support groups so that they can take part in a new sport together if they are worried about going it alone; the support of the group can boost the women's morale in other areas of their lives, too. They advertise in local libraries, health centres, sports centres and newsagents to see if they can gather together a group of like-minded women to meet on a regular basis and support each other. Some groups decide to engage perhaps a fitness expert, someone who knows about exercises and anatomy, or yoga, or massage; other groups arrange for experts to give them lectures or come and work for the group; some arrange their own sessions at a leisure centre to avoid being involved in the general mêlée of the sports hall.

The Women's Health and Reproduction Rights Information Centre (WHRRIC – address in Appendix II) issues details about women's groups; unfortunately they rely upon people giving them up-to-date information and cannot guarantee that what they give out is accurate. However, if you are interested in either joining or forming a group of any description, it is a good idea to let the Centre know.

A group's moral support can be crucial. One of the most difficult problems facing large women who want to be active is the attitude of other people. Many large children, for example, enjoy dancing but are put off it by the ridicule of others, not only of their peers but also adults, who should know better, and a pleasant pastime and beneficial exercise are thus denied them. Memories of childhood ridicule often make a woman hesitate to try again later, but they can take heart from the Roly Polies dancing group. As they explain in their book *Fat, Fit and Fruity* (how's that for a positive attitude?), they were originally brought together as a one-off act but proved so popular that they have appeared regularly ever since, especially on the Les Dawson television show. All the women are large and all are extremely fit: they could not pursue their dancing career if they were not. The Roly Polies are living proof that large women can be fit and can also be neat and nimble on their feet. Rather than being mocked for their size, they are greatly admired for their energy and fitness.

'Wet' sports can be ideal for large women; indeed fat can be a distinct advantage in the water. As Jonathan King put it in a 1982 article in the *San Francisco Chronicle* ('Why diets don't work'), if you throw a pound of butter into a swimming pool it will float like a cork, whereas a lump of lean meat will sink. The same applies to body fat: the more you have of it, the easier you will find it to float. In fact, just for the sake of experiment, you can estimate what proportion of body fat you are carrying by floating on your back in the swimming pool after filling your lungs with air. Blow the air out and see what happens. Those whose bodyweight includes more than 25 per cent fat will float easily. A healthily fat woman with 22–23 per cent body fat can usually float while breathing shallowly. At 15 per cent (which is low for a woman but normal for a man) the body will usually sink slowly, even with a lungful of air, and at 13 per cent you will sink easily, even in salty sea-water (though the density of Utah's salt lakes or the Dead Sea might give you some support). However, this floatability can be a disadvantage: if you want to take up diving, you may need to use a lot of extra weights.

There can be practical problems with a watersport like canoeing: I find it extremely difficult to get a canoe large enough for me to sit in to paddle and often have to resort to the kind that you kneel in. On the other hand, I thoroughly enjoy wind-surfing.

Wet sports can be exciting and exhilarating but some women prefer some gentle exercise swimming. Swimming is ideal for large women and is probably the best way of toning up the whole body whatever your size or sex. It is particularly good for older people or those who are really out of shape because it does not put too much stress on the spine or joints. Like any other exercise, you should start gradually and aim to build up in gentle stages to a steady quarter-of-an-hour of non-stop swimming when the effect will be aerobic and will strengthen your heart and dramatically improve your circulation. Swim smoothly, with a relaxed stroke and a regular pattern of breathing. Take time to wind down at the end of a session: finish with a gliding lap, then eliminate any build-up of carbon dioxide in your system by exhaling deep breaths under water. Follow this with a quiet walk in the shallow end to stop your legs feeling a little shaky when you leave the pool.

It can sometimes be difficult to find a public pool which is not so crowded that continuous swimming is almost impossible, but early mornings can be a good time, and many pools set aside certain times during the day or evening for more serious swimmers. Your local YWCA might well have a swimming pool and can advise you when it will be more or less free of children.

Do not be deterred by the thought of appearing in public in a swimsuit. Invest in one that fits well, in a colour and style that suit you. If you feel good in it, why care about other people?

Swimming is one of four types of exercise advocated by Ann Harper in *The Big Beauty Book*. She also mentions cycling, skipping and 'pep-stepping'. Pep-stepping is a quick walk that maintains a steady speed and develops a 'peppy' rhythm, and is recommended in preference to jogging. Every time a runner's feet hit the ground, especially on unforgiving surfaces, the whole body receives a shock which is equivalent to up to three times the body's weight, and many joggers or runners sustain quite serious knee injuries as a result. Pep-stepping or walking briskly is just as good for the heart and other systems as jogging, without the risk of damaging the knees.

Skipping is a typical childhood activity which most of us have enjoyed and it is a cheap, readily available form of exercise which can be carried out in your own back garden. Invest in a decent skipping-rope, with ball-bearings in the handles, and make sure it is the right length, i.e. twice the distance from your armpit to the floor. Skip by bouncing on the balls of your feet and avoid landing flat-footed. Start gradually: spend the first session getting used to the idea and play some music to help you get the feel of the underlying rhythm of skipping. Work up gradually to a couple of minutes of non-stop exercise and aim eventually for a quarter-of-an-hour, which should be very much a long-term goal. Wear rubber-soled shoes and a good, supportive bra: bouncing breasts can be very uncomfortable.

Bicycling is another childhood activity which is well worth trying again as an adult if you used to enjoy it. You may find that you are rusty and that your legs ache at first, but you will not have forgotten how to cycle even if you have not been near a bike for years. Make sure the bike fits you, that the seat is comfortable, and that the balls of your feet are comfortable on the pedals. The saddle height should allow you to pedal with your legs almost straight but not fully extended.

Bowling is another possibility, as long as you do not have back problems, but even better is golf, which involves plenty of walking but can be enjoyed at your own pace. Pacing yourself is important with any exercise: you should be pleasantly tired by it, not exhausted. Short periods of exercise lasting perhaps fifteen or twenty minutes four or five times a week, especially in the earlier part of the day, will be enough to make you feel much better: you will have more physical and mental energy, look better, sleep better, relax more easily and be less prone to illness and disease. For those who find it difficult to fit regular exercise into their schedules, a slight change of routine can help: walk instead of using the car for a short trip, or get off the bus a few stops earlier and walk the rest of the way, or use the stairs rather than the lift. It all helps.

The cheapest, easiest and most convenient exercises of all are gentle stretching and appropriate rhythmic breathing to improve fitness generally. The first step is to learn how to stand with a good posture: unslouch your spine by relaxing your shoulders, tucking in your bottom and then imagining an invisible string drawing the top of your head towards the sky. The string is attached to the crown of your head, which should prevent you from jutting out your chin or tucking it in tightly like a guardsman on drill. Many large women are ashamed of their big breasts and tend to round their shoulders to disguise the bust, but good posture, with the shoulders relaxed rather than either rounded or thrust back in military style, will not draw unwanted attention to the bust.

For gentle exercise, which will both relax and tone your body, stand with good posture with your feet slightly apart. Breathe slowly and deeply into your abdomen and out again, for a few breaths. Relax. Very gently and slowly, turn your head from one side to the other, then allow it to drop slowly on to one shoulder and roll it, very gently, over to the other shoulder and back again. Do this three times. Never let your head drop quickly or suddenly forwards or backwards.

Now work on your tense shoulders. Let your arms hang freely and use your shoulder muscles to circle your arms gently, first backwards three or four times and then forwards, until the tension is relieved.

Next comes the stretching. Stand straight, and raise both arms above your head. Gently stretch up with the right arm, straightening the elbow and reaching the fingers towards the sky. Feel the stretch all the way down your right side to the waist. Then do the same with your left hand.

To relax and stretch the feet and ankles, stand straight and support yourself on the back of a chair or the top of a kitchen unit. Stand on one leg and point the other, then slowly flex the foot so that your toes point to the sky. Stretch it out again, repeat six times, and then change legs. Another exercise, still supporting yourself, is to stand on one leg, flex the toes of the other foot and slowly rotate it from the ankle, first in one direction and then the other.

All these are good for warming up before you start more serious exercising. If you want to be more strenuous, it is worth checking with your doctor that there is nothing fundamentally against you going ahead, and it is sensible to have your blood pressure checked anyway. Always start any new exercise gradually, giving your muscles a chance to adjust to the demands you will make on them, and always have some kind of warm-up before serious exercising and a wind-down afterwards.

Do try to progress in due course to something more ambitious than simple flexing and stretching, because a firm framework of muscles makes a lot of difference to how you feel and look, whatever your size. Stand naked in front of a long mirror, think about your posture, and tighten your muscles – especially those of the abdomen and buttocks. Don't you immediately look a better shape and more alive? There is no need to weigh yourself as long as your body is properly toned by exercise, but if you do step on the scales you might find that your weight has not decreased noticeably although your body looks a great deal less flabby and your vital statistics have altered.

Aerobic and isometric exercises are the most efficient for general fitness and probably the best for tuning the muscles and improving your shape, but activities as simple as walking, stretching, or even walking up and down stairs are beneficial and will increase your sense of well-being, which is what it is all about.

The ability to relax is also important to your physical and mental health, whatever your size or degree of fitness. We use basic relaxation and awareness exercises in the workshops as part of the process of helping women to listen to their bodies and to feel 'good inside'. There are two relatively simple exercises which women can do in a group under guidance, or with the help of a friend, or on their own with the aid of a tape-recorder. The sound of a calm, soothing voice taking you through the different stages of the exercises is therapeutic as well as instructive, and you might like to make your own tape of the instructions exactly as given here, or ask a friend or a member of the group to read them out, very slowly so that everyone has time to let herself get in touch with different parts of her body and be aware of any messages her body needs to give her.

Pay special heed to allowing plenty of time for a relaxed person to absorb your words. In deep relaxation, people are absorbing information without actively listening, and they need ample time to accept the suggestions and sensations at their own gentle pace. Your recording or reading should therefore include all the long pauses and repetitions set out in the text. Make every comma a pause, and every set of dots long enough for several slow breaths.

For all these kinds of exercises, give yourself plenty of time and space. Create a pleasant atmosphere in the room, perhaps using candlelight, and make sure it is comfortably warm. Wear loose, comfortable clothing so that nothing distracts you from relaxing. Use the first exercise perhaps once a day, regularly in the morning or last thing at night, or whenever you feel tense. Some people like soft music in the background; personally I find that less helpful, but do whatever is best for you.

Lie on your back on the floor and make yourself comfortable. You will find, perhaps to your surprise, that you will not need cushions to be able to relax.

Let your arms lie naturally along the floor and let your legs and feet feel relaxed and unflexed. Become aware of your breathing. Just let yourself breathe deeply, and slowly, in and out, and allow yourself to concentrate on your breathing. Breathe deeply into your abdomen. As you breathe, allow the tension to go out as you breathe out . . .

Be aware of the parts of your body which are touching the floor. Let yourself feel the weight of your body on the floor. As you breathe out, allow yourself to relax and to touch the ground more . . .

Now place your hands on your belly, just below your belly-button, and when you breathe in allow your breath to go down to your stomach so that your hands rise slowly on the in breath and fall on the out breath. Let all your breath out of your lungs each time . . . Breathe slowly like this for several breaths, making sure your stomach lifts your hands each time . . .

Now become aware of any tension in your body. Start with your feet. Feel the tension in your feet. As you breathe in, exaggerate the tension, allow your feet to tense right up and then, when you breathe out, relax your feet and imagine you are breathing out all the tension from your feet. Do this ten times: when you breathe in, exaggerate the tension, and let the tightness and tension go as you breathe out . . .

Now concentrate on your legs: let yourself feel the tension in your legs, your calves, your knees, your thighs. As you breathe in, exaggerate the tension, really tense the muscles, and as you breathe out relax the tension. Let it go with the breath from each part of your legs. Do this a few times . . .

Now your pelvis: allow yourself to feel the tension in your pelvis. Breathe in and, as you do, exaggerate the tension. And then breathe out, release it, breathe all the tension out, and do this several times more . . .

Continue with the same pattern of tension and release for your belly, your chest, your shoulders, arms, neck, head and face, exaggerating the tension in each part and then releasing it as you breathe in and out. Finally relax the whole body by just breathing deeply and slowly as you did at the beginning, feeling your weight on the floor.

The second exercise helps you to be in touch with your body and feel good about it by paying more attention to its messages. Start as for the first exercise, lying comfortably on the floor and breathing evenly, and deeply, in and out, slowly and rhythmically. Focus on your breathing. Feel your body touching the floor, feel your weight on floor . . .

Let your awareness travel slowly and gently over your body: allow yourself to feel the sensations of your body . . . Without judgement, note which parts attract you . . . and which parts are calling for attention or nourishment . . .

Take the first part of your body which calls for your attention. Put your hands there and imagine you are breathing into that part. Now explore any physical sensations you feel there . . . Are there any emotions connected with that part of your body? Don't censure: allow the first thing that comes to your mind, and trust it . . . Are there any memories you find there? . . . Is there any other information this part of your body wants to give you? . . . If so, accept it . . . Now ask yourself, what does this body part need? What is it saying? Can it tell you anything about yourself? . . . Explore how you can give this part of your body what it needs . . .

When you feel quite ready, open your eyes, allow your awareness to come back into the room . . . In your own time, slowly, very slowly, turn on your side and sit up slowly, in your own time.

This exercise needs time and practice. Some people find fantasy quite difficult and need to practise if they want to pursue it, whereas others with a good imagination find it relatively easy quite quickly. It involves using intuition and becoming more aware of our bodies, and taking time to give them positive, caring attention. Various ways of nurturing ourselves may suggest themselves during the exercise: they could be practical ideas or simply a decision to be more aware of that part of the body and to nurture it more.

Both these relatively simple relaxation and awareness exercises can be done by women on their own, with a friend or in a group. Some of the books in the Bibliography give alternative techniques or you can devise your own. It is very much a matter of what suits the individual. The golden rules are: don't force yourself into anything; don't grit your teeth and make yourself do something you are not happy about; give yourself plenty of time and space – and give it a try. Like countless people before you, you might find it very enjoyable.

I have suggested that, if you want to practise more strenuous forms of exercise or sport, it is wise to check with your doctor first but, as we have seen, many large women have problems in dealing with doctors and are wary of consulting them. They need to come to terms with this by identifying the difficulties and learning how to handle them. This becomes easier when you have regained some of your self-confidence and are more aware of the true facts about size and health.

The doctor's consulting room is another place where assertiveness, rather than aggression or extreme passivity, plays its part. The main point is that you should be able to tell the doctor clearly what your problem is, and then make sure you ask all the questions you want to ask and really listen to and remember the answers. Before you visit the surgery, write down what is wrong: for example, instead of talking about 'pain', be ready to describe what sort of pain, where it is, and how often it occurs. Be very clear in your own mind about any anxieties you have in connection with this pain and make a point of discussing them with the doctor. Make a list of what you want to know and then talk it through with a friend beforehand. Ask the friend to go with you, partly for moral support, partly as an extra pair of ears. The friend is not there to act as your spokesman but to listen and to collect any information that the doctor gives you. Very often you will find that, after the visit, your friend has heard information which you simply failed to listen to or ignored because of your emotional state or preconceptions. Take your list of questions into the surgery to make sure that you can ask all the questions you think you need to ask. This is particularly important for a patient-group like large women, who may have to face prejudice in the medical profession because of their size.

Doctors are busy people, but it is important that you should understand what the proposed prescription will do for you. In 1976 the following simple questions about prescriptions were suggested in *The Lancet* by Dr Andrew Herxheimer, and your doctor should be happy to answer them:

What kind of tablets are they and how can they help me? How should I take them? How do I know that they are working? How important is it that I take them and what might happen if I don't? Do they ever cause trouble or have side-effects? Can I drive after taking them, or take other medicines with them, or drink alcohol? How long must I continue with them and what should I do with tablets I don't need? Will I need to see the doctor again and, if so, what will the doctor want to know?

If the risks or side-effects are unacceptable to you, remember that it is your body and your choice. The same applies, of course, with more traumatic treatment like surgery. Do bear in mind the doctor's possible prejudices against your size but don't let that distract you from the original point of your visit.

7

IN YOUR OWN FASHION

Nutrition and exercise are fundamental to health, and a healthy woman looks good. She can enhance her appearance by wearing clothes which really suit her and give her confidence.

We ask women to come to the workshops wearing (or bringing) clothes they feel good in and also clothes which were a mistake. We look at them, try them on, and try them on other women in the group, noticing how important proportion is. That is true for all people, regardless of size, but it is a factor often overlooked in the case of large women. The assumption by clothes manufacturers, society in general, other women and the women themselves is that they cannot look good anyway, so any attempt at dress sense is a hopeless task. However, once the women get together in groups and take a good look at clothes, discussing them among themselves, they usually come up with some marvellous ideas that can change their attitudes to clothes completely. And because they are a group, they are supportive of each other rather than negatively critical. At first they tend to lack confidence in their dress sense, as in everything else, but when they actually try clothes on and experiment, and look at outfits that fit and suit them well and others that they realize are mistakes, then they begin to recognize how the elements of proportion can make an outfit suit them when it does not suit other women in the group or, conversely, how their own 'mistake' outfits can look attractive on other women.

Dress sense is not about size: it is about visual effect. The visual impact you make is based upon the proportions and shape of your body – the framework for clothes. The art of good dressing is to understand the framework and to clothe it to best effect.

In women of all sizes there are four basic shapes. First, there is the figure-of-eight: the classic Marilyn Monroe or Mae West shape in which the bust and hips are similar in size and there is a definite indentation at the waistline. This is the easiest figure to dress, whatever your size.

Next is the traditional pear shape of most British women, in which the upper part of the body measures less in its circumference than the bottom half. Quite often there is a difference of one or two sizes between bust and hips: for example, you might have a size 18 bust and size 20 or 22 hips. This shape can be difficult to dress but it is not impossible.

Then we have the barrel shape, in which the upper torso (between neck and waistline) is fairly short and is broader than the lower torso – wide in the shoulders, short in the waist and probably top-heavy in profile. The barrel-shaped woman's waist is often thicker than her hip measurement and most of these women have delectable thighs and legs.

Figure of 8

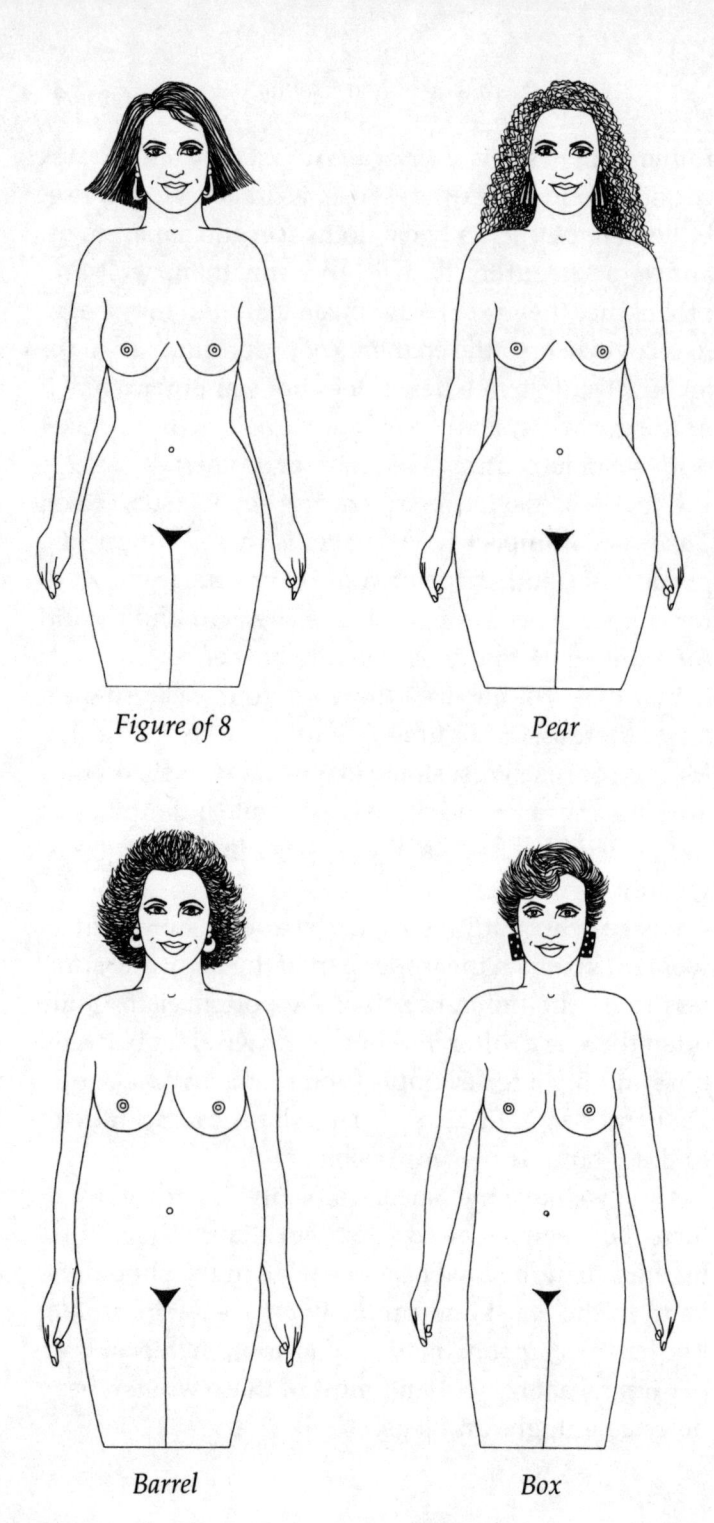

Pear

Barrel

Box

Finally there is the box shape, which is generally broad all the way round and more or less straight up and down without much of a waist. The general outline is in straight lines rather than curves.

It is important to identify your shape, for the same clothes will not necessarily look good on all these different outlines.

Stand in front of a full-length mirror (which may have been a nightmare for you in the past) and look at yourself without critical judgement to assess your shape. At the same time, look at the vertical proportions of your body. In your imagination, divide your body into four sections: the top is from the top of your head to the nape of the neck or the shoulders, the second from the nape to the waistline, the third from the waistline to where the thighs begin and the fourth from the thighs to the tips of the toes. You can take a photograph of yourself in a swimsuit or leotard and draw horizontal lines across to define the four sections, as the illustration on p.140 suggests.

If the upper part of the torso appears shorter than the lower part, you are high-waisted; conversely, you are long-waisted if the proportions are reversed. If these two sections together (that is, your torso from the nape of the neck to the top of the thighs) are shorter in length than your legs from thigh tops to toes, you can call yourself leggy, and if they are longer you are short-legged.

All these proportions can be altered by the clothes you wear. Styles can make your waist appear higher or lower, for example, or hemlines can be raised or lowered, or matching tights can give the appearance of torso and legs being of equal length when they are not. Take a look, too, at your head in proportion to the rest

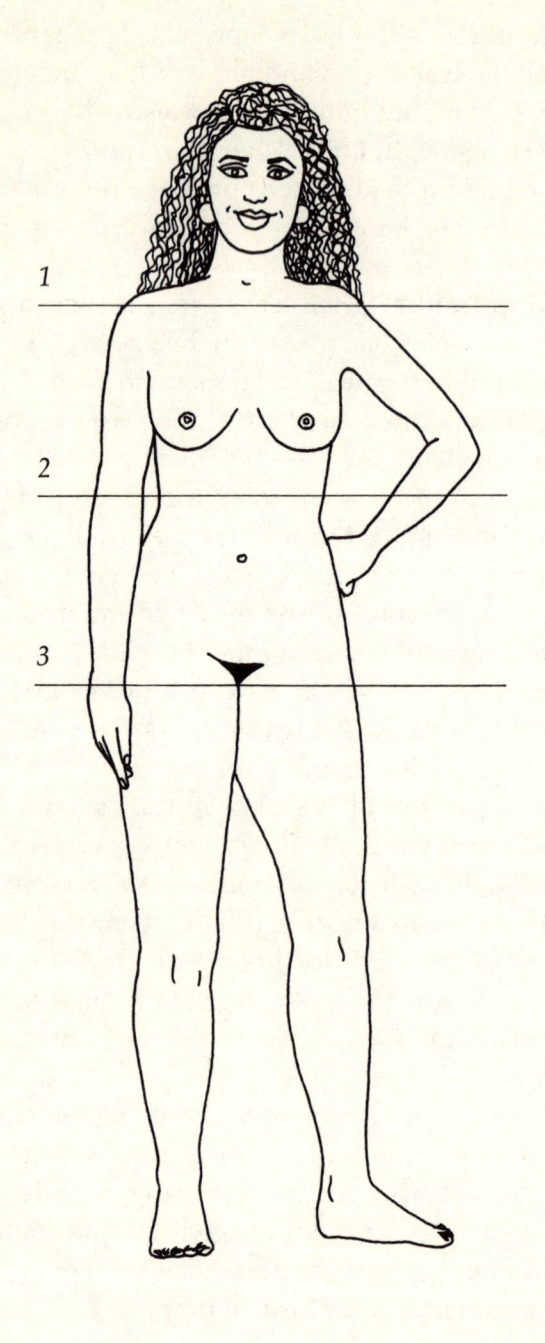

of your body and see whether it looks small or large. To what degree does it share the attention with the upper part of your body? This will give you a clue about whether you need to make your head appear larger or smaller by having a short, cropped hairstyle or something more bouffant and wide. The actual shape of your face will also play a part in determining the best hairstyle. Experiment if you have long hair by taking it up, or see how a fringe might affect your total look and proportions.

Try on a variety of different clothes to see their effect as you stand in front of the mirror. Like bodies, clothes have lines drawn across them by collars, waistbands and belts, by the finishing line of a jacket, by the hem of a dress or skirt, by shoulders and shoes. Work out individually a balanced distance between the feet and the hem, for instance, and the hem to the line at the waist or hips, and from there to the shoulderline. These are the proportions any woman who wants to look good and feel comfortable in her clothes needs to assess when putting her wardrobe together.

Different styles suit different shapes. A shirt-dress with a fuller skirt can look good on pear shapes and boxes. Blouson styles with a billowy top or ample sleeves can give more size at the top to a pear-shaped woman, who might also benefit from shoulder pads to balance the difference in size between top and bottom. Drop waistlines are good for box shapes to break up the rigid symmetry. The line at which the drop waist comes is important and is individual for different women.

Something as simple as the shape of a neckline can make all the difference to an outfit, and I take a selection of necklines to the workshops so that women can try them out. Whether you wear a heart-shaped neckline, a square, a wide V, a narrow V, or perhaps a polo-neck, turtle-neck, simple round, crew or slash neckline, you will find that the shape can change the appearance of your face and shoulders and can be crucial to the balance of the whole outfit.

Shoes also affect the proportions of an outfit: some look better with flat shoes, others with high heels. The colour and texture of clothes are vital, too: an outfit in one colour can look particularly good, or might be improved by wearing toning tights, or enhanced by a combination with other colours which either tone or contrast with it.

There is one rule I would make for all women, whatever their shape or size: never buy anything that is too small. Tight clothes do not look good on anybody, and it is better to buy something slightly larger and take it in or not to buy it at all. This becomes easier once you have the confidence not to be embarrassed by the size label in your clothes.

When trying on clothes, move in them and look at yourself all the way round. Take someone with you who will give a second opinion and will look at you from different angles that you cannot see for yourself. A good fit is imperative, of course. Signs of a poor fit are straining buttons, tightness under the arm, sleeves that expose the wrist, or ridges across the back of a jacket. If there is enough fabric to let down the sleeves and everything else fits, fine, but if not look for something else. Make sure that the waist of the garment actually sits on your natural waistline and is not too high or too low. You should be able to sit and bend comfortably in skirts and trousers without popping buttons or stretching seams or feeling in any way restricted. You certainly should not have to hold your breath in order to zip up the garment and you should be able to walk easily rather than awkwardly in it. On the other hand, beware of bagginess, which can be unsightly and can make all of us look much larger than we are.

Deciding what suits you is one thing; next come the very real problems of finding what you want in the shops – in your size. In the workshops we share information about where good-quality, well-cut clothes can be bought, but the search can be long and arduous. I have found that the designs of the 1920s, 1930s and 1940s suit me very well: they have a cut and style which skims over the body and flares out into a beautiful hemline and they are cut on the cross so that the fabric (usually crepe or something soft) swings rather than clings. They generally have quite neat shoulder-pads without 'Dallasty' excesses, and neat bodices with dropped waistlines and perhaps full, panelled skirts. After years of torment trying to find good-looking clothes, particularly for special occasions, I have gathered together about six original dresses from that period which I adore wearing. I find them sometimes in antique shops, though the prices are always increasing, or in flea markets; they are not easy to track down, but it is worth trying. Debbi Thompson's book *Glad Rags: The Best Secondhand Clothes Shops in London* has proved helpful but some of the addresses may be out of date.

Having found the styles that suited me, I have had patterns cut from some of my favourites so that they could be made up in new fabrics of my choice. I have also bought various books with sketches and photographs of clothes of the period and had patterns made from them as well. For example, Jan Peacock's *Fashion Sketchbook 1920–1960* gave me some lovely ideas for evening wear, day dresses, coats and underwear, and some of the bridal wear could be converted for evening wear. In Ann V. Tyrrell's book *The Changing Trends in Fashion: Patterns of the 20th Century* there are pictures of a man and a woman each in dress of the period or year, starting in 1901 and finishing in 1970, and each picture is accompanied by a description of the kind of material and accessories. There are patterns with instructions for enlarging them so that someone with experience can trace the pattern from the book and size it up. Another dressmaker's delight is Janet Arnold's *Patterns of Fashion: English Women's Dresses and Their Construction, 1860–1940* which is a little more exotic and includes information for metric conversion, pattern-cutting and dressmaking techniques for the period. There are miniature patterns in the book which an experienced person would be able to adapt. Many of the designs are from clothes in the Museum of Costume.

Maggie Lane has produced a delightful book, *Oriental Patchwork: Elegant Designs for Easy Living*, which is full of quite loose-fitting oriental garments like beautiful kimonos, Turkish trousers, kaftans, jackets, dresses, Indian pants and tabards, all of which can be adapted by good pattern-cutters and dressmakers. Betty Foster, whose dressmaking series have been broadcast on independent television, has written several books about adapting or creating patterns and there are other books on pattern-cutting which are invaluable for larger women who have difficulty finding clothes they like. Those with some experience can buy a multi-pattern and work out the difference between two sizes on it, then step up by the same amount to the size they want as long as it is not more than two sizes larger than the largest on the multi-pattern, and as long as they take into consideration the length of the garment from nape to waist and from waist to hem. (Winifred Aldrich's book on *Metric Pattern Cutting* is a good source of information.)

There are many people who have the skills to make up a pattern from a drawing or picture of a dress you particularly like and think may suit you. If you see a magazine or catalogue picture of a garment which is not in your size, take it along to a good pattern-cutter or dressmaker and see what they can do for you. Charges will vary depending on where you live, of course. Local technical colleges usually have a fashion and design department and can be very helpful if you discuss the possibility of being put in touch with someone appropriate. Those who are good at dressmaking themselves have the advantage and quite often become skilled simply because they despair of finding suitable clothes in the shops. With luck you will have such a treasure in your support group.

Men's clothes shops can be a great source of delight to the larger woman. She can find beautiful T-shirts and perhaps jeans, jackets, woollens, or even the perfect pair of shorts. There is a chainstore for large men which can be very useful.

Underwear is as important as the rest of the outfit. Avoid tight-fitting, cutting underwear which pulls the body in to such an extent that it has to bulge out elsewhere. If you wear a bra, a well-fitting one is essential and you must try it on before buying because sizes can vary tremendously from style to style. Comfort is important. Some women like underwired bras, though personally I find them dreadfully uncomfortable. Choose a style you like and then take at least three sizes into the changing room to try them on. Move in them: stretch your arms above your head, bend down, fold your arms, throw them wide apart (if the cubicle is big enough!) and close them again. Move in all the ways that you can think of to make sure the bra remains comfortable.

All-in-one undergarments need to hug the figure gently rather than clad it in iron so that it bulges out on either side. One of the dangers of all types of girdle or panty-girdle is that they tend to push out an unsightly roll of flesh below them. It is wiser to wear just a good-fitting pair of briefs or possibly panty-briefs for light control, providing they fit well and avoid that roll. Teddies, which combine French knickers with a slip top, can look very attractive on large women but they might be difficult to find.

For some reason the manufacturers believe that large women do not want the flamboyant, pretty underwear they produce in smaller sizes, and trying to get a pair of frilly French knickers or a sexy bra can be a real difficulty for a woman of large proportions. Tights can be a nightmare, too: their crutch is usually several inches below your own and the only way you can walk is by keeping the tops of your legs and your knees together – very uncomfortable, I can assure you! Many large women opt for stockings instead and then have the problem of finding suspender belts which are comfortable and which have long enough elastic to meet the stocking-tops.

Shoes can also be difficult to find. Large women do not necessarily have long, large-boned feet but very often they have broad feet and if they are tall their feet will be long as well. (Our skeletal structure is usually in proportion and it used to be common for a gynaecologist to ask you how big your feet are because that gives an indication of the size of your pelvis and it can be judged whether you might have difficulties in childbirth.) Most shoe manufacturers might go to size 7 or 7½, or even an 8, but many of the shoes are cut very narrow so that large women have difficulty getting pretty shoes which fit.

At the moment there are very few manufacturers who offer a good range of large styles. It is time we let them know what we want because if we don't tell them they will never know.

8

FIGHTING BACK

As large women gain more confidence in themselves and recognize that the old myths and the accusations which are flung at them are not true, their experiences are affirmed by other women in similar situations. And, once they realize that they are *not* greedy people, that they do *not* eat more than others, that they are *not* slothful, frumpy and out of control, then they are ready to challenge the perpetrators of the oppression they have suffered.

Women at Big and Beautiful workshops discuss their experiences in small groups, finding out what individuals have done about prejudice or would like to do about it. Some of the ideas which are generated they find exciting and energizing, particularly the realization that they can take charge of their own lives and actually do something about the people and institutions who have ignored or vilified them. This is very much where assertion, rather than aggression, needs to be practised.

One area in which to begin is clothes. Large women

are all too used to being told by a shop assistant, 'We haven't got anything in *your* size, madam.' Instead of shrinking and withdrawing, women are encouraged to ask questions. Why haven't you got that style in my size? Could I speak to your buyer/department supervisor/shop manager? Can you give me the address of your head office so that I can write and complain about there being nothing here in my size? If none of us complain, then how can we expect the manufacturers to appreciate the extent of the problem?

Slowly, large women are beginning to have an effect on the clothing industry, but there is still much scope for enterprising firms to make sports clothes, underwear and general wear for larger women in all walks of life. For example, dress designer Jennifer Carr Jones of Chichester sells a range of classic clothes from size 10 to 20 by mail order and finds that 'people seem to have got larger over the years.' In an article in her local paper, she is quoted as saying: 'The sizes we sell most of are 14 and 16, but we actually sell more size 20 than size 10. I realized when I started several years ago that bigger women have a rough time of it where fashion is concerned, so we keep the fashion line going throughout the size range. They have just as much fashion flair as everyone else and this gives them a chance to indulge it.'

In 1988 one of the large mail-order companies woke up to the fact that many of its customers (probably the majority, as so many larger women dislike going into clothes shops) needed larger sizes and began to offer a good selection of styles available right through the size range from 12 to 24 and in some cases to 30 – proving that the same style can be equally suitable for large and small women provided the proportions are right. The catalogue featured media personality Gloria Hunniford, and the copywriters had the grace to admit: 'Women don't come only in smaller sizes – so why should fashion?' Exactly! What is more, the catalogue also featured Valerie Roussez, describing her as: 'A lovely young model, with the Marilyn Gauthier Agency in Paris, she is in great demand for her size 18 figure. She makes public what many admit in private: that big is beautiful. She models our new collection for evening, and underlines our commitment to a fashion policy which breaks the size barrier.'

Manufacturers need positive encouragement from us. Whenever we find a dress that we like but which is not in our size we should write to the manufacturer saying how much we like the design and how we wish it was made in our size too. The same applies to shops: if you see clothes you like, write to the managing director of the shop explaining what it is you like and suggesting that you would buy it if it were available in your size. Explain that there are a lot of large people around and you are sure that, like you, they would buy the clothes if only they were available. Write to manufacturers who do actually produce good-quality clothes which fit and have style, and express your appreciation; encourage them and offer suggestions for designs you think would particularly suit you. Even businesses respond to appreciation. Tell people what you would like: make your voice heard. If enough of us do that, then people will begin to act as well as listen.

Despite recent improvements, society's attitudes in general are not changing quickly enough. There are still many ways in which large people can be embarrassed by their needs being thoughtlessly neglected. As we have seen, restaurants, cinemas, trains, buses and aeroplanes where the seating is fixed can be a nightmare for large people. Safety-belts on planes can be a problem and although some airlines now offer large people the extensions they carry for pregnant women, would it not be better to make the belts larger anyway? Large people, men and women, cannot be that much in the minority on the passenger list – or is it the case that we travel less because we are less confident and therefore less obvious? We should let them know. Write to the head office, be it of an airline, chain of restaurants or cinemas or a bus company, and explain your difficulties to the managing director (always go to the top). Say that you would use their facilities more if they were more attractive and made more comfortable for you. If an airline is helpful in terms of seat-belts, commend it; if not, complain and offer suggestions. In commercial organizations profits talk, and we need to convince these people that there is a profit for them in satisfying our needs. Point out the extent of their potential market.

In recent years car manufacturers have been altering their designs in an attempt to attract female customers but they have quite failed to tackle the problem of the design and position of driving seats in relation to the wheel. As any large or pregnant woman can tell you, many cars are so cramped that it is very difficult for them to find a comfortable position behind the wheel, or in some cases to get behind the wheel at all. Reaching the pedals safely can be another problem, even worse for shorter women (who sometimes have to crane their necks to see over the wheel anyway). Tall people have their problems too. And car seat belts, which are uncomfortable for most mature women, can be unwearable for a large or pregnant one. That means there must be a fairly high percentage of car users who are dissatisfied with car design. Let them say so!

I urge women to complain constantly when the service they are offered is not appropriate or adequate, rather than to blame themselves and apologize for their existence. Make sure that everyone from the shop assistant to the managing director knows what we want. If we do not ask for it, then we are never likely to get it. That means writing letters stating our needs clearly; it means complaining about inadequate space in public places and alerting industrial designers to their lack of imagination and consideration.

It also means tackling the media to help open the eyes of the general public to its prejudices. Write to fashion editors, women's page editors and the general editors of newspapers and magazines to tell them that we are large women readers and we want to see big clothes on big models, we want to see large sizes included in fashion features as a matter of course. We do not want to be treated as odd and separate but as part of the whole range. Point out that nearly half the women in this country are size 16 or more and that, once they have proved they will cater for *all* women, then the sales of their publications will increase.

Get the same message across to programme makers and extend it well beyond the fashion features. Whenever we hear or read an item (usually tucked away as a passing reference) about an injustice to large women, then we need to write and insist that such incidents are dealt with more clearly. If there are features on dieting, the dangers of dieting should be pointed out and the benefits of being large should be incorporated rather than the persistent portrayal of fashionable thinness.

We can also complain about advertisements, especially those for dieting placed incongruously near features on luscious food recipes. Suggest to the media which display the advertisements that perhaps they should think more seriously about them. Complain to the advertisers about images in which large women are portrayed as unacceptable and only thin women can be beautiful. Question the lack of positive role models within the visual arts, and demonstrate that beautiful women do not have to be thin. Challenge the way in which all the language of success involves being thin: a company that is doing well is described as efficient, economical and 'lean', or is made more efficient by 'paring it down to the bone'. Such descriptions imply that large is inefficient, slow and stodgy and we need to confront that kind of linguistic image.

We need to speak out and take up space rather than try to shrink, contract, be smaller and pretend we are something we are not. We are winning slowly, in practical areas, but we still need to change people's attitudes to large women, to dispense with the notion that there is something wrong with them merely because it is fashionable to be thin.

Women need to use their voices: they need to be heard. I hope that this book will go some way towards giving the world an insight into what it is like to be large in a society where the ideal image is thin; I hope it will open your eyes to the passive prejudice and thoughtlessness which cause almost as much damage as active ridicule. I hope above all that it will convince large women that they are not greedy or lazy or 'a problem' but that, like anyone else, they are individuals with a great deal to offer. Let them have the confidence to be themselves, and to love and care for their bodies, and let them stop wasting their energies on trying to conform to the ideal image of today. Then they can turn those energies to much more important matters – and *then* they will be admired and accepted for themselves. Harness your energy and channel it: there is nothing you cannot do.

APPENDICES

I

NUTRITION

VITAMINS AND MINERALS: THEIR ROLES IN THE BODY

VITAMINS

VITAMIN A (RETINOL)	Important for normal growth in children; necessary for good vision and growth of bones and teeth; essential for healthy skin, eyes, hair and mucous membranes.
VITAMIN B_1 (THIAMINE)	Necessary for proper functioning of heart, nervous system and muscles; essential for growth; required to obtain energy from food (part of enzyme system releasing energy from carbohydrate foods).
VITAMIN B_2 (RIBOFLAVIN)	Necessary for healthy skin; essential for building and maintaining body tissues; concerned with sensitivity of eyes to light (it is itself easily destroyed by light); participates in protein metabolism.
VITAMIN B_5	Required for health of skin and hair; essential for growth of all tissues.
VITAMIN B_6 (PYRIDOXINE)	Important for healthy teeth and gums, the health of the blood vessels, red blood cells and the nervous

	system; necessary for converting food to energy (participates in metabolism of amino acids, fatty acids and protein synthesis); necessary for synthesis of adrenal hormones.
VITAMIN B_{12} (CYANOCOBALAMIN)	Essential for healthy blood formation (needed for normal development of red blood cells, prevention of pernicious anaemia); contributes to health of nervous system and to proper growth in children; contains cobalt.

OTHER B VITAMINS

FOLIC ACID	Essential for healthy blood formation (in conjunction with vitamin B_{12}) and for integrity of intestinal tract and digestive system.
CHOLINE	Essential for correct functioning of the liver, particularly with regard to fat metabolism.
INOSITOL	Working in conjunction with choline, essential for correct functioning of liver and metabolism of fat.
NIACIN	Necessary for converting food to energy; aids the nervous system; needed for maintenance of appetite and for healthy skin.
BIOTIN	Necessary for integrity of skin and mucous membranes; also for health of red blood cells and cardiovascular system.
VITAMIN C (ASCORBIC ACID)	Essential for healthy teeth, gums and bones, and the building of strong body cells and blood vessels; participates in adrenal gland functions, use of some protein elements, absorption of iron; prevents scurvy; daily dietary needs relatively large.

VITAMIN D (CALCIFEROL)	Necessary for strong teeth and bones; helps in utilization of calcium and phosphorus to form healthy bones and teeth; prevents rickets.
VITAMIN E (TOCOPHEROL)	Acts as an anti-oxidant of polysaturate fats in tissues; essential for the integrity of red blood cells; protects other nutrients such as vitamin A from destruction by oxidation.
VITAMIN K (PHYTOMENADIONE)	Essential for prothrombin synthesis (which is involved in the body's system for controlling blood clotting) in the liver.

MINERALS

Calcium	Essential for formation and maintenance of strong bones and teeth; controls the response of nerves and muscles to stimuli; needs vitamin D to be effective.
Chromium	Thought to be involved in metabolism of carbohydrates and fats needed for production of insulin.
Copper	Essential part of various body enzymes; involved in formation of red pigment of blood (haemoglobin).
Iodine	Essential to metabolism; contributes to the formation of thyroxin (active principle of the thyroid gland) which chiefly regulates metabolic energy.
Iron	Necessary for keeping the blood healthy: forms part of the red pigment of blood that carries oxygen from lungs to other parts of body and takes the waste product, carbon dioxide, back to the lungs.
Magnesium	Assists in making proteins and keeps muscles in tone.

Manganese	Essential for normal growth, reproduction, bone development and functioning of the nervous tissue; thought to be involved in maintenance of blood sugar levels.
Phosphorus	Needed with calcium to build and maintain bones and teeth. Helps provide energy.
Selenium	Appears to be able to protect body from effects of oxidation of polysaturates; works in parallel with vitamin E.
Sodium and Potassium	Go hand in hand to work on body cells; in balanced proportions they maintain nerve signals and muscle contractions; also help acid balance of body fluids.
Zinc	Necessary for growth and maturity of reproductive organs; helps maintain healthy skin; is thought to help taste and flavour perception

Other trace elements, such as nickel, tin, vanadium, cobalt, silicon, boron, are thought to be essential for health but their functions are poorly understood. They are active ingredients in body cells, blood and organs.

MAJOR SOURCES OF VITAMINS

VITAMIN A	Liver, kidney, eggs, milk and dairy produce, fish liver oils, dark green leafy vegetables, yellow vegetables (containing carotene).
VITAMIN B_1	Yeast, liver, pork, peas, whole-grain bread and cereals, wheat germ, sunflower seeds.
VITAMIN B_2	Milk (rich source), yeast, offal (liver, kidney), lean meat, poultry, fish, eggs, cheese, fresh green leafy vege-

	tables, yellow vegetables, bread and cereals.
VITAMIN B$_6$	Meat, liver, vegetables, whole-grain cereals, molasses, sunflower seeds, cod, fresh salmon.
VITAMIN B$_{12}$	Lean meat, fish, milk.
VITAMIN C	Citrus fruits, fresh green vegetables, broccoli, peppers, cabbage, new potatoes, fruit juices.
VITAMIN D	Substantial amounts in cod liver oil; small amounts in eggs and certain fish (salmon, tuna, etc.); produced by action of ultraviolet rays on substances in the skin: the sunshine vitamin.
VITAMIN E	Fresh green vegetables, whole-grain cereals, wheatgerm, vegetable oils, milk, peanuts.
VITAMIN K	Fresh leafy vegetables, egg yolks, molasses.

FOODS HIGH IN REFINED CARBOHYDRATES

Ready-to-serve breakfast cereals
White bread
Pancakes
Cakes and icings
Biscuits
Pies
Rolls and muffins
Sandwich buns
Crackers
Pretzels
Macaroni
Noodles
Spaghetti
Sweet rolls
Doughnuts and waffles
White and instant rice
Cream sauces and soups
Sweet pickles
Snack foods (cheese puffs, onion rings etc.)
Ice cream
Milk shakes
Sherbet
Tinned/frozen fruit in syrup
Sweetened apple sauce
Syrups and sweet sauces
Jams
Sweets
Chocolate
Jelly
Puddings

Custards
Sweetened yogurt
Instant breakfast
Hot chocolate
Ovaltine
Soft drinks
Fruit drinks
Lollipops

Iced lollies
Beer
Wine
Spirits
Liqueurs
Brandy
Cordials
Squash etc.

FOODS HIGH IN SUGAR

Sweetened and sugar-coated cereals
Cakes and icings
Biscuits
Pies
Bran muffins
Crackers
Sweet rolls
Doughnuts
Ice cream
Sherbet
Fruit, tinned or frozen, in syrup
Sweetened apple sauce
Chocolate sauce
Other sweet sauces and syrups
Jams
Sweets, including:
    Chocolate bars

Boiled sweets
Peppermints
Cough sweets
Instant breakfasts
Sweet pickles
Sweetened yogurts
Jelly
Puddings
Custards
Hot chocolate and chocolate milk
Milk shakes
Canned or frozen fruit drinks
Squash
Soft drinks
Iced lollies
Dessert wines and cordials

II

USEFUL ADDRESSES

FASHION SHOPS

The Base: Rushka Murganovic, 55 Monmouth Street, Covent Garden, London WC2H 9DG (01-240 8914)

Big Clothes, 81a Boundary Road, London NW8 (01-722 1127)

Designer Plus, 156 Lower High Street, Stourbridge, West Midlands (0384 390877) (Within Second Sense)

Dickins & Jones: Sixteen Plus, 224 Regent Street, London W1A 1DB (01-734 7070)

Elaine, 80 Bedford Place, Southampton (0703 228 242)

Escorpion, 296 Station Road, Harrow, Middlesex HA1 2DX (01-863 2855)

Evans Collections, Press Office: 214 Oxford Street, London W1N 9DF (01-636 8040). 118 outlets nationwide.

Forgotten Woman, 24 Marylebone High Street, London W1N 3PE (01-935 4159). Other shops elsewhere.

Harrods: Eighteen Plus Shop, Knightsbridge, London SW1X 7XL (01-730 1234)

Long Tall Sally, 21 Chilton Street, London W1M 1HG (01-487 3370)

Magnum, 19 Southgate Street, Winchester, Hants (0962 52980). Other shops elsewhere

Marks & Spencer: Plus Range (to size 24), selected stores. Information from 366 Baker Street, London W1A 1DN (01-935 4422)

Selfridges: Your Size, Oxford Street, London W1A 1AB

(01-629 1234). Other stores elsewhere.

LINGERIE AND NIGHTWEAR
Can-Can, 188 Grays Inn Road, London WC1X 8EW (01-833 3531). Mail Order and shop.

Lingerie by David Napier (mail order sizes 10–24, free catalogue) Salgrave House, PO Box 14, Somercotes, Derby (0773 836000)

GENERAL MAIL ORDER
Brian Mills, Commercial Road, Sunderland SR9 9AA (091 565 0650). Catalogue includes Emphasis up to size 30.

Carr Jones, 51 South Street, Chichester, West Sussex (showroom) (0243 788523 for brochure)

Emphasis, J.M. Centre, Old Hall Street, Liverpool L70 1AB (051 235 3037)

Extra Plus, Grattan plc, Freepost, Bradford, West Yorkshire BD99 2YE (0274 575511)

Fashion Extra, PO Box 1600, London W8 7HD (01-437 9744)

PATTERNS
Betty Foster, Scope House, Western Road, Crewe, Cheshire CW1 1DD (0270 587594)

Leslie Fogel, 5 South Molton Street, London W1Y 1DH (01-493 2541)

Vogue Pattern Service, New Lane, Havant, Hants PO9 2ND (0705 486221)

SHOES
Tall & Small departments of selected branches of Saxone, Lilley & Skinner, Magnus, J. D. Williams.

SPORTSWEAR
Shore Marine, 130 Appin Road, Argyll Industrial Estate, Birkenhead, Mersey L41 9HH (051 666 1237). Boating/sailing wear to 54in bust. Mail order or from ships chandlers.

SWIMWEAR
Triumph International, Arkwright Road, Swindon, Wilts SN2 5BH (07939 22200)

ORGANIZATIONS
National Association to Aid Fat Americans (NAAFA), PO Box 43, Bellerose, NY 11426, USA

Women's Health and Reproduction Rights Information Centre, 52–54 Featherstone Street, London EC1H 8RT (01-251 6580)

MAGAZINES
BBW (Big Beautiful Woman), Suite 214, 5535 Balboa Blvd, Encino, Ca 91316, USA

Radiance, PO Box 31703, Oakland, CA 94604, USA

SHOPPING IN AUSTRALIA

BRISBANE
Big Impressions, Shop 15, Redcliffe Arcade, Redcliffe (284 0307)

Design Catwalk Studio (after hours by appointment), 15 Watland Street, Springwood (208 6897)

Sandra's Big Girl Fashions, Budget & Fashion Labels (Personalised Service), Cnr. Pacific Highway and Harris Road, Underwood (841 1173)

SYDNEY
Apples Boutique, 9 Redcliffe Avenue, Wahroonga (487 2704)

Desirable Habits, 156 Waterloo Road, Greenacre (740 5226)

Vicki's Reflections, 4 Minto Mall Shopping Center, Minto (603 6536)

ADELAIDE
Daff's Boutique :(Hand-printed and appliquéd originals), 242 Kensington Road, Marrayatville (332 4052)

Supersizes, The Gallerie Shopping Centre, Ground Floor, Adelaide 20 Gawler Pl. (223 2608) and Glenelg 2 Sussex (294 5122)

PERTH
Turning Point, Nollamara Shopping Center, Hillsborough Drv., Nollamara (349 8314) and Shop 14, Maylands Shopping Centre, Guildford Road, Maylands (272 2078)

Big Girl Sizes, 5 Springpark Road, Mdlnd (274 3903) and 900 Albany Highway, East Victoria Park (361 3701)

MELBOURNE
Michell's Larger Sizes and Maternity Wear (size 8 to 28), 408 Burwood Road, Hawthorn (819 1358)

14 Plus Fashion (size 14 to 26), Keys Street Level, Peninsula Centre, Frankston (781 4092)

Leading Lady (size 16 to 30), The Big Girl's Shop, 1 Duncans Road, Werribee (741 4032)

Joan's Little Shop (Maggie T stockists size 12 to 24), 85 Puckle Street, Moonee Ponds (375 3865) and 1033 Mt. Alexander Road, Essendon (379 2757)

III

BIBLIOGRAPHY

BOOKS USED IN PREPARING THIS BOOK

Andelin, Helen: *Fascinating Womanhood* (out of print)

Banks, Morwena, and Swift, Amanda: *The Joke's On Us: Women in Comedy from Music Hall to the Present* (Pandora, 1987)

Bennett, William, and Gurin, Joel: *The Dieter's Dilemma* (Basic Books, New York, 1982)

Cannon, Geoffrey, and Einzig, Hetty: *Dieting Makes You Fat* (Sphere)

Chapkis, Wendy: *Beauty Secrets: Women and the Politics of Appearance* (The Women's Press)

Chernin, Kim: *The Hungry Self: Women, Eating and Identity* (Virago, 1985)

Chernin, Kim: *Woman Size: The Tyranny of Slenderness* (The Women's Press, 1983)

Chetwynd, S. J., *et al*: see Howard, Alan

Friedman, Rita: *Beauty Bound* (Columbus Books)

Goodhart, Robert S., and Shins, Maurice (eds): *Obesity* (Febiger Press)

Harper, Ann, and Lewis, Glen: *The Big Beauty Book: Glamour for the Fuller Figure Woman* (Sidgwick & Jackson)

Howard, Alan (ed.): *Recent Advances in Obesity Research* (Newman Publishing, 1975)

Hutchinson, Marcia Germaine: *Transforming Body Image: Learning to Love the Body You Have* (The Crossing Press, 1985)

Melville, Joy: *The ABC of Eating: Coping with Anorexia, Bulimia and Compulsive Eating* (Sheldon Press)

Millman, Marcia: *Such a Pretty Face: Being Fat in America* (Norton, 1980)

Morgan, Marabel: *The Total Woman* (1973)

Orbach, Susie: *Fat Is a Feminist Issue: A Self-Help Guide for Compulsive Eaters* (Paddington Press, 1978)

Roberts, Nancy: *Breaking All the Rules* (Viking)

Roberts, Nancy: *Woman and Food* (Pluto)

Roly Polies: *Fat, Fit and Fruity* (W. H. Allen, 1986)

Rowe, Marsha, (ed.): *The Spare Rib Reader* (Penguin)

Schoenfielder, Lisa, and Wieser, Bob: *Shadow on a Tightrope* (Aunt Lute Book Company, Iowa City)

Worcester, Nancy, and Whatley, Mariannett: *Women's Health: Readings on Social, Economic and Political Issues* (Kendall Hunt, Iowa)

SUGGESTED FURTHER READING

Dixon, Anne: *A Woman in Your Own Right: Assertiveness and You* (Quartet)

Donald, C. M.: *The Fat Woman Measures Up* (Rag Weed Press)

Dowling, Colette: *The Cinderella Complex: Women's Fear of Independence* (Fontana)

Eichenbaum, Luise, and Orbach, Susie: *What Do Women Want?* (Fontana); *Understanding Women* (Penguin)

Ernst, Sheila, and Goodison, Lucy: *In Our Own Hands* (Women's Press)

Norwood, Robin: *Women Who Love Too Much* (Arrow Books)

Phillips, Angela, and Rakusen, Jill (British eds): *Our Bodies Ourselves: A Health Book By and For Women* (Boston Women's Health Book Club)

FASHION, PATTERN-CUTTING AND DRESSMAKING

Aldrich, Winifred: *Metric Pattern Cutting: A Unique Completely Metric Method for Designing Beautiful Clothes* (Bell & Hyman, rev. ed 1979)

Arnold, Janet: *Patterns and Fashions: English Women's Dresses and Their Construction, 1860–1940* (Macmillan/Drama Book Publishers, New York, 1972)

Foster, Betty: *Betty Foster's Dressmaking Course for Fashion That Fits* (Independent Television Books, 1982)

Foster, Betty: *Creating Fashion* (Macdonald & Co. with Thames Television, 1983)

Foster, Betty: *Adapting to Fashion: Creative Fashion for a Basic Master Pattern* (Macdonald & Co. with Thames Television, 1980)

Lane, Maggie: *Oriental Patchwork: Elegant Designs for Easy Living* (Bell & Hyman/ Charles Scribner, 1978)

London, Liz E., and Adams, Anne H.: *Colour Right, Dress Right: The Total Look* (Dorling Kindersley, 1985)

Peacock, Jan: *Fashion Sketchbook, 1920–1960* (Thames & Hudson, 1977)

Thompson, Debbi: *Glad Rags: The Best Secondhand Clothes Shops in London* (Wildwood House, 1984)

Tyrrell, Ann V.: *The Changing Trends in Fashion: Patterns of the Twentieth Century* (Batsford)

NUTRITION

Brown, Sarah: *Healthy Eating Cook Books: Raw Food* (Dorling Kindersley for Sainsbury's, 1986)

Dimbleby, Josceline: *Salads for All Seasons* (Woodhead Faulkner for Sainsbury's, 1981)

Elliot, Rose: *Book of Salads* (Fontana)

PAPERS AND ARTICLES CONSULTED

Brown, Catrina, and Forgay, Don: 'An Uncertain Well-being: Weight Control and Self-Control' (*Healthsharing*, Winter 1987)

Cahnman, W. J.: 'The Stigma of Obesity' (*Sociological Quarterly*, vol. 9, 1968)

Canning, H., and Muir, J.: 'Obesity – Its Possible Effects on College Acceptance' (*New England Journal of Medicine*, vol. 275, 1966)

Downey, Alison: 'Fat is a Feminist Issue' (*Womanwise*, Spring 1983)

Ernsberger, Paul: 'Is it Unhealthy to be Fat?' (*Radiance*, Winter 1986)

Farquhar, D. L., Griffiths, J. M., Munro, J. F., and Stevenson, F. (Eastern General Hospital, Edinburgh): 'Unexpected weight regain following successful jaw-wiring' (*Scottish Medical Journal*, vol. 31(3), July 1986)

Ferriman, Annabel, and Merritt, John: 'Scandal of the Slimming Clinics' (*Observer*, 13 March 1988)

Frisch, Dr Rose E.: 'Fatness and Fertility' (*Scientific American*, March 1988)

Garrow, J. S., and Gardiner, G.T.: 'Maintenance of weight loss in obese patients after jaw-wiring' (*British Medical Journal*, vol. 282, 14 March 1981)

Hodgkinson, Neville: 'Obesity: Research blames metabolism' (*Sunday Times*, 28 February 1988)

Jenkins, Tina, Smith, Heather, and Burford, Barbara: 'Fat Liberation' (*Spare Rib*)

Keys, Dr Ancel: 'Seven Countries: A Multivariate Analysis of Coronary Heart Disease and Death' (Harvard, 1980)

King, Jonathan: 'Why Diets Don't Work' (*San Francisco Chronicle*, 17 May 1982)

Norsigian, Judy: 'Dieting is Dangerous to Your Health' (*The Network News*, May/June 1986)

Priest, Ruth: '10 Reasons Not to Diet' (*Radiance*, Spring 1987)

Rand, Colleen S. W., and Kuldau, John M.: 'Stress and Obesity' (*Stress Medicine*, vol. 1, 1985)

Ronay, Egan: 'Mrs Spratt, All is Forgiven' (*Sunday Times*)

Russell, Janice: 'Eating Disorders and Sexuality' (*Healthright*, vol. 6, no. 3, May 1987)

Smead, Valerie S.: 'Anorexia Nervosa, Buliminarexia and Bulimia: Labeled Pathology and the Western Female' (*Women and Therapy*, vol. 2, 1983)

Sternhall, Carol: 'We'll Always Be Fat, But Fat Can Be Fit' (*MS* magazine, May 1985)

Stunkard, A. J., et al: 'Social Factors in Obesity' (*J. Am. Med. Ass.*, vol. 192, 1965)

Wills, Judith: 'Weird and Not So Wonderful Ways to Lose Weight' (*Prima*, June 1988)

Wooley, Susan and Orland W.: 'Obesity and Women: A Closer Look at the Facts' (*Women's Studies International Quarterly*, vol. 2, 1979)

Yudkin, J.: 'Obesity in Society' (*Biblthca Nutri Dieta*, vol 26, 1978)

INDEX

actuarial charts 14, 49, 64, 80–1
  'scientific' basis of 15
acupuncture 67
airlines, explaining difficulties to 151
advertising: aims of 69
  complaining about 153
  ideal image in 30, 97
aggression 112
alcohol 117, 120
Aldrich, Winifred: *Metric Pattern Cutting* 145
American Journal of Nursing 66
American Surgeon, intestinal bypass article 65
amino acids 45, 116
anaemia 84
Andelin, Helen: *Fascinating Womanhood* 49
anger 112
  expressing 100, 102
Anne, Queen 56
anorexia: incidence in US 54
appetite: control centre 72
  depressant 45, 46
Arnold, Janet: *Patterns of Fashion . . . 1860–1940* 144
assertion 108
  practising 148ff.

babies: criticism of large 23
  risk of premature 84
Baker Brown, Dr 60
Banks, Morwena (and Swift, A.): *The Joke's On Us* 31, 33, 35, 36
beauty, standards of 106
Bennett, William (and Gurin, J.): *The Dieter's Dilemma* 70

bicycling 125, 126
bingeing 76, 106
blood pressure, high 80, 82, 83, 120, 128
Blundell, Dr John 70
body: becoming aware of 102–3, 109, 120
  listening to 8, 105
  neglecting 105, 108
  talking about 106
body-building 26
body image: poor 90–1
  visualization techniques 102
body shape 53–4, 137, 139
body size: acceptance of 8–9, 94, 104
  in art 56, 57
  dissatisfaction with 19
  eating patterns and 92
  factors affecting 13
    hereditary 85
  historical perspective 17, 30, 55ff., 94, 97, 98
  Mediterranean attitudes 55
  misjudging by voice 29–30, 34
  prejudices against 9
  as sign of fertility 55
  as sign of wealth 53–4
  and social/economic opportunities 18
  society and 19–20
  stabilizing factor 27
  talking about 19
body temperature: control centre 72
bowling 126
bras 146
breast milk 87
breasts: cosmetic surgery on 58, 61
  good posture and 127

self-consciousness over 61
British Psychological Society 70
Bron, Eleanor 35
Bunbry, Grace 113
bust-binding 58

Cahnman, S. J.: 'The Stigma of Obesity' 52
calories, using up 13
cancer, risk of 84
Canning (and Muir): 'Obesity – Its Possible Effects on College Acceptance' 53
Cannon, Geoffrey (and Einzig, H.): *Dieting Makes You Fat* 71
car manufacturers, complaining to 151–2
carbohydrates 116–17
   good sources of 117
   refined 117, 120
      food high in 161–2
career: effect of size on 15, 16, 27, 97
Carr Jones, Jennifer 149
catecholamine neurotransmitters 78
Chapkis, Wendy: *Beauty Secrets . . .* 27
Chernin, Kim: *Woman Size: The Tyranny of Slenderness* 18
Chetwynd, S. J. 17
child psychologists 25
children: and 'acceptable' size 25
   parents' protection of 23–5, 60–1
   and support group 123
   teasing 20, 25
   see also daughters
cholesterol 83
Clinical Research Centre, Harrow 63
clothes 105, 141–3
   buying 107
      asserting yourself 149
      antique 143–4
      mail order 149–50
      from men's shops 146
   cutting patterns from 144–5
   discussing 100–1, 136ff.
   for exercising 41, 130
   experimenting with 100–1, 137, 141
   imported 40
   loose 24
   19th-century 56
   necklines 101, 141–2
   pitfalls to avoid 39
   problems at work 15
   ranges for larger women 40
   ready-to-wear 7
   sizes 25, 39, 41, 93, 143
   society and 19
   see also sportswear
clothes shops 40
   complaining in 101–2
clothing industry 41, 149, 150
complaining, methods of 149, 151–2
compliments 106
controlled imagery 110
Cook, Beryl 113
Cornell University: bingeing study 76

corsets 57, 98
cosmetics, 'hiding' behind 26
criticism: challenging assertively 112
   difficulties coping with 27–8
   discussing 149
   from family 14
   of large-breasted women 61
   in workplace 14–15

dancing 21
daughters: dressing 24
   pressures on 60
   sexually acceptable 26
depression 43
diabetes 80, 82
diet: changing to nutritional 105
   eating balanced 115–16
      constituents 118
   and osteoporosis 88
   rich/poor fallacy 51–2
dietary aids 11, 83
dieticians 25
dieting 7–8
   aims of 70
   bingeing after 75–6
   constituents of weight lost 71
   effects: on behaviour 72
      on hypothalamus 73–4
      on metabolism 71
      on set point 75
      of severe 86
   follow-up studies 78–9
   forgetting about 104
   maintaining will-power 44, 68
   obsession with 48
   physiological changes during 70–1
   plateau 78
   sedentary dieter 72
   side-effects 71–2
   stopping burning fat 78
   stress and 43
   support during 16
   talking about 106
   weight gain after 10, 62–3, 72, 75, 98
diets 18
   basis of 79
   children on 25
   discussing 105
   effect: of 'forbidden' food 78
      of liquid protein 83
      of low-carbohydrate 83
      of near-starvation 71
   failure of 94–5
   improved 80
   for pregnant women 84–5
   slow-loss 78
Dinesen, Isak 61
discrimination: in college acceptance 53
   discussing 97
   in the family 101
   by health promotion organizations 41
   and lack of confidence 83
   by medical profession 41–2
   in public places 20
   and stress 42–3

Index

at work 14–15
diuretics 45, 46, 77
diving 124
doctors 25
   dealing with 133–5
   moral support when visiting 134
   see also discrimination
Dunn Nutrition Unit, Cambridge 13
Duromine 45
dress sense 137
   see also clothes

'E' numbers 120
Earth Mother image 29–30
Eastern General Hospital, Edinburgh 63
eating, compulsive 16
   after dieting 75–6
   healthiest eaters 84
   internal/external cues 70
   in public 16
   after stopping smoking 121
   second helpings 24
   uncontrollable 73
   see also food consumption
eating disorders 9–10, 15–16, 90ff.
eating habits: control over 16
   nutritious 8
eating patterns: fat/thin 70
   inappropriate 91, 92
Einzig, H. *see* Cannon, Geoffrey
El Saadawi, Nawal: *Spare Rib* interview 59
Emberg, Bella 36–7
emphysema 84
energy: from fats 117
   from proteins 116
   usual source of 117
   when dieting 71, 74, 77–8
entertainment, large women in 30ff.
Ernsberger, Paul: *Radiance* article 82, 83, 85
exercise: discussing 98–9
   effect of excessive 86
   for muscle tone 99
   and osteoporosis 88
   for suppleness 99
exercise bikes 41
exercise classes 21
exercises 21, 122, 126, 127–8, 130
   relaxation and awareness 102–3, 109, 129, 130–2
   alternative techniques 133
   see also swimming
Extra Special magazine 40–1

fashion: changes in 97
   complaining about features on 152–3
fashion industry: bias of 22, 94
   and ideal image 11
fat: of average 18-year-old 86
   and bad health 112
   beneficial influence 68
   effects: of distribution 82
   of excessive 82–3
   on pregnancy 86–7
   estimating proportion of 123–4
   excess 17
   use during famine 68
'Fat Politics' 28
fatness: definition of 15–16
   and fertility 86–7
   obsession against 18
   as psychological shield 26
fats (lipids) 117
'felt image' 111
female circumcision 59–60
feminist movement: attitudes in 28
   backlash against 50
Ferret, Eve 35–6
fitness 16, 41, 43ff., 115, 121ff.
'fitness' organizations 11
Fitzgerald, Ella 113
food: additives in 120
   buying 118–20
   cooking methods 116
   explaining constituents 116
   goodness of natural 115–16
   for nutritive diet 105
   obsession with 90ff.
   processed 116
   vitamins in 118
food consumption 16
   and body size 13–14, 15–16
   changing patterns of 94–5
   dieting and 70
   discussing healthy 119
   recording 92
   rituals associated with 95
food cravings 91
Forde, Florrie 30
Foster, Betty 145
Friedman, Rita: *Beauty Bound* 27, 49–51, 53, 56, 58–9, 61
Frisch: 'Fatness and Fertility' 86–7
Frusemide 45

Gardiner, G. T. 63
Garrow, J. S. 63
gastric bypass 63–4, 65
gastric operations: side-effects 65
gastric partitioning 63, 64
gastroplasty 63, 64, 67
Gerontology Research Center 81, 82
girdles 146
golf 126
Gravely, Norma J.: 'Sexist humour' 31–3
greed 16
   disproving 92–3
Greeks, ancient: 'thinness' drug 56
guided imagery 110
guilt 79
   as incentive to slim 44–5
Gurin, Joel *see* Bennett, William

hair loss 71
hairstyles: determining best 141
Handl, Irene 35
Harper, Ann 113

Index

The Big Beauty Book 125
health 41, 43ff.
  discussing 98
  effect of bingeing/purging on 77
  effect of stress on 97
  problems with 15
  risks from overweight 80
health clubs 44
health programmes 18
  clothes for 41
'health' organizations 11
heart attacks 82
height/weight ratio 7, 80–1
  see also actuarial charts
Herxheimer, Dr Andrew: *Lancet* article 134
Hird, Thora 35
Hodgkinson, Neville: *Sunday Times* report 13
hormones 72, 73
humour: bias in 31–3
hunger signals 70
Hunniford, Gloria 113, 150
Hutchinson, Marcia: *Transforming Body Image* . . . 102
hypertension 83
hypothalamus 72, 73–4, 76, 77, 86
hypnotherapy 67
hypothermia 73

ideal image: attaining 57–8
  eating to maintain 69
  conforming to 8, 25
  historical perspective 10–11, 112
  current 17
  reducing to 106
illness: underweight and 84–5
  use of fat during 68
imagination: developing/using 102, 109, 110, 111, 113
intestinal bypass 63–4, 65, 66
intragastric balloon 67
insurance risk 14–15
ITMA 'Fat Person' 34

Jacques, Hattie 34, 35
jaw-wiring 62–3, 98

Kavanagh, Ted: *The ITMA Years* 34
Keys, Dr Ancel: weight study 81
King, Jonathan: *San Francisco Chronicle* article 123

Labhart, Dr: *South African Medical Journal* article 65
Lane, Maddie: *Oriental Patchwork: Elegant Designs* . . . 145
large/jolly stereotype 31ff.
laxatives, effect after bingeing 77
laziness 16
Lepoff, Laurie: *Shadow on a Tightrope* 28
  weight loss surgery article 65–6
little-girl look 50–1
love, test of 26
lung cancer 74

Margolyes, Miriam 35
massage: engaging expert 122
  therapeutic 107
maternalism 87
  attitudes to 54–5, 56
Mayer, Jean: *Obesity* 85
mealtimes, set 70, 115
media: bias in 94, 97
  complaining to 102, 152–3
  effect on personalities 113
  and ideal image 11
  and the large woman 17
  role models in 30
  stereotyping 34ff.
    in America 36
  use of advertisements 97
  see also entertainment
medical profession: attitude to overweight 83, 100
men: historical role 51
  obesity/class factors 52
  and prepubescent image 50–1
  self-awareness in 19
  threat to security 32
menarche: average age of 87
  trigger for onset of 86
menopause: weight averages during 85–6
menstrual disorders 73
  thinness and 86
metabolism: effect of smoking on 74
  personal 13–14
  lower rates of 13
  slowing down 71
milk 118
Millman, Marcia 56
minerals 117, 159–60
models: current US trends 50
  first for 'fuller figure' 113
  rejecting image of 106
Morgan, Marabel: *Total Woman* 49
mortality 81–2
  in thin people 84
  weight and 84
muscle tone: exercising for 99, 128–9
  loss of in dieting 71–2
  massage for 107

narcolepsy 73
National Institute of Health 80
  on weight-loss surgery 66
Noppa, H. 82
Norman, Jessye 113
nutrition 115–16
nutrients, essential 116–18

obesity: criteria for determining 80–1
  factors affecting in Britain 54
  health risks 82
  incidence in US 52, 54
  as 'killer disease' 80–1
  medical profession and 42
  mental health and 83
  man/woman differences 52–3

Index

morbid 64–5
social status and 51ff.
suicide rates 85
Oberver: slimming clubs investigation 45–6
oestrogen 85–6
and bone replacement 88
Orbach, Susie: *Fat is a Feminist Issue* 9, 26, 75, 91
osteoporosis 84, 88–9
overweight *see* obesity

pampering yourself 99
panty-girdles 146
Peacock, Jan: *Fashion Sketchbook 1920–1960* 144
'pep-stepping' 125
personality 33
personal appearance 15
and self-confidence 22
pin-up postcards 57
pituitary gland 72, 73
Pizzey, Erin 30
planes: safety-belts 151
seats 20
posture, good 127
prejudice, social 10–11, 19–20
on overeating 14
prescriptions, questioning 134
Priest, Ruth: *Radiance* article 74
Prima magazine: jaw-wiring article 62–3
surgery article 66–7, 68
principal boys 30
proteins 116
puberty, delayed/early 73
public houses 20
public places, consideration in 97
public transport 20, 151
purging: effects of 77
talking about 106

Rayner, Claire 30
Rea, Marjorie 31, 33
Reading, Bertice 113
regurgitation 56
relaxation: importance of 129–30
techniques 109
see also exercises
restaurants 20, 151
Revelle, Roger 87
ribs, surgical removal of 58
Roberts, Nancy: *Breaking All the Rules* 38, 39, 113
role models 30
author as 114
complaining about 153
positive 113
therapist as 29
Roly Polies: *Fat, Fit and Fruity* 123
Romans, weight regulation 56
Ronay, Egon: *Sunday Times* article 46
Roussez, Valerie 150
Royal College of Physicians, obesity report 75

salt 120
Sanderson, Tessa 113
seatbelts 97, 151
self-affirmation 111
self-confidence, gaining 106–7, 108
self-esteem 43, 83, 91, 94
self-indulgence 16
disproving 92–3
self-image: fragile stage 114
improving 91ff.
changing to positive 103
self-love 12, 107
learning 109
and stress 43
self-nourishment 12, 107, 120
self-worth, building up 108
selfishness 99
sex life 19, 27, 29
sexism, challenging 9
sexual functions, control centre 73
sexuality, shield against 26–7
shoes 142, 147
shorts 41
silicone implants 58
Sims, Joan 35
sizeism 17–18, 28–9
skin: effect of smoking on 120
reduction in elasticity 71
skipping 125–6
sleep: control centre 72
disorders 73
slimming clubs/clinics 11, 44–7
slimming industry, harm done by 83
smoking: effects: on mineral/vitamin needs 120
on set point 74
stopping 120–1
snacks 121
Social Factors in Obesity 52–3
social groups 32
large women in 33
society, attitudes of: and age 19
dealing with 108
discussing 101–2
effect of 96
'spare tyre' 82
spontaneous imagery 110
sports: participating in 21
reluctance to join centres 98–9
'wet' 123–5
sportswear 41
availability/choice 21
finding suitable 98–9
stays 57
stress 42–3, 97, 197
stretch-marks 71
'stomach stapling' 63
long-term side-effects 67
Stunkard, Dr Albert J. 74
sugar 117, 120
food high in 162
support groups 123
surgery 11, 47, 62ff.
on breasts 61
criteria for patient selection 64

Index

motives behind 58–60
  questioning 135
  to restore longevity 65
  statistical comparisons 66
sweets, avoiding 121
Swift, Amanda *see* Banks, Morwena
swimming 99, 124–5
swimsuits 24, 41, 125

T-shirts 41
tapeworms 67–8
Taylor, Dr Vincent 67
thinness: attitudes in US 54
  obsession with 18–19
  recognizing as passing fashion 106
  resistance to 55
  risks associated with 84–5
  sign of emancipation 54–5
thirst, control centre 72
Thompson, Debbi: *Glad Rags* . . . 144
tights 147
tracksuits 41
trousers 41
tuberculosis 84
Twiggy 48, 97
Tyrrell, Ann V.: *The Changing Trends in Fashion* . . . 144

ulcers 84
underwear 145–6
uniforms, company provision of 15
uterine cancer 80

Veblen, Thorstein 53
'victim syndrome' 79–80, 108
vitamin psychosis 83
vitamins 117–18, 157–9
  major sources of 160–1
vomiting, self-induced 77

walking 98
Wallace, Julie T. 37
water balance, control centre 72–3
weighing, obsessive 104, 106
weight: age factor 81
  and bone strength 88
  contemporary obsession with 48–9
  discussing 105
  eating patterns and 92
  effect on mortality rate 81–2
  genetical control of 74
  medical profession's attitude to 41–2, 100
  men/women ranges 82
  and menarche 88
  'normal' 9–10
  increases in 48
  set point for 72–3, 74
  superstitions 55–6
  and wealth 53–4
weight gain: as protection 26–7
  and self-image 27
weight loss: before activities 94
  forgetting about 104, 105
  maintaining after dieting 75, 78
  as sexual threat 16–17
  surgery *see* surgery
Weight Watchers 44
Weldon, Fay: *The Life and Loves of a She-Devil* 37
Whitbread, Fatima 113
Windsor, Barbara 34–5
Windsor, Duchess of 53
windsurfing 99, 124
witch superstitions 55–6
Wolf, Louise: 'Weight Loss Surgery . . .' 65–6
women: changing eating habits 95
  effects of undernourishment 87–8
  emotional difficulties 42–3
  food obsessions 90ff.
  historical role 51
    subordination of 49ff.
  image of the ideal 51–2
  large/thin differences 19
  use of fat reserves 86, 87
Women's Health and Reproduction Rights Information Centre 122–3
Worcester, Nancy: *Fat Phobia* 52
Women and Food 95
workplace: image in 30
  prejudice in 41
  problems in 14–15
workshops 8, 93, 95, 96, 102–3, 104, 110–11, 120–1, 122
Wood, Victoria 32, 33, 38
Wooley, Susan 75, 84
  Glamour magazine survey 48–9
Wooley, Susan and Orland 17, 64, 65

yoga 99
  engaging expert 122
'yoyo syndrome' 83–4